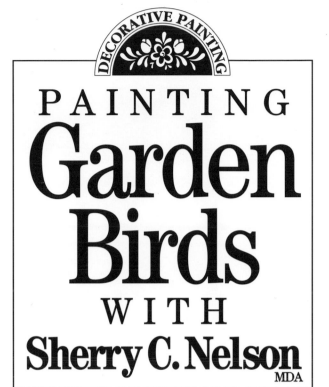

DECORATIVE PAINTING

PAINTING
Garden Birds
WITH
Sherry C. Nelson
MDA

PAINTING
Garden Birds
WITH
Sherry C. Nelson
MDA

NORTH LIGHT BOOKS

Cincinnati, Ohio

Painting Garden Birds With Sherry C. Nelson MDA. Copyright © 1998 by Sherry C. Nelson. Manufactured in China. All rights reserved. The patterns and drawings in this book are for the personal use of the decorative painter. By permission of the author and publisher, they may be either hand-traced or photocopied to make single copies, but under no circumstances may they be resold or republished. It is permissible for the purchaser to paint the designs contained herein and sell them at fairs, bazaars and craft shows.

No other part of this book may be reproduced in any form or by any electronic or mechanical means including information storage and retrieval systems without permission in writing from the publisher, except by a reviewer, who may quote brief passages in a review. Published by North Light Books, an imprint of F&W Publications, Inc., 1507 Dana Avenue, Cincinnati, Ohio, 45207. (800) 289-0963. First edition.

Other fine North Light Books are available from your local bookstore, art supply store or direct from the publisher.

04   03   02   10   9

Library of Congress Cataloging-in-Publication Data

Nelson, Sherry C.
    Painting garden birds with Sherry C. Nelson. — 1st ed.
        p.   cm.
    Includes index.
    ISBN 0-89134-771-2 (pb)
    1. Birds in art. 2. Painting—Technique. I Title. II. Title: Decorative painting
ND1380.N45   1998
751.45'4328—dc21   97-36341
                CIP

Edited by Kathy Kipp and Dawn Korth
Production edited by Marilyn Daiker
Designed by Angela Lennert Wilcox
Cover illustration by Sherry C. Nelson MDA

The photograph on page 127 is used by permission of Deanne Fortnam. All other interior photographs and step-by-step photography is by Deborah Ann Galloway.

METRIC CONVERSION CHART

TO CONVERT	TO	MULTIPLY BY
Inches	Centimeters	2.54
Centimeters	Inches	0.4
Feet	Centimeters	30.5
Centimeters	Feet	0.03
Yards	Meters	0.9
Meters	Yards	1.1
Sq. Inches	Sq. Centimeters	6.45
Sq. Centimeters	Sq. Inches	0.16
Sq. Feet	Sq. Meters	0.09
Sq. Meters	Sq. Feet	10.8
Sq. Yards	Sq. Meters	0.8
Sq. Meters	Sq. Yards	1.2
Pounds	Kilograms	0.45
Kilograms	Pounds	2.2
Ounces	Grams	28.4
Grams	Ounces	0.04

ACKNOWLEDGMENTS

Deborah Galloway is the other half of my painting business, The Magic Brush. This book is as much hers as mine. She took the many step-by-step photos, worked through the inevitable problems with film processing, and kept her smiling good humor through it all. She lets me use (and enjoy) her extensive collection of photos from over twenty years of wildlife photography, and she shares some of them here in this book. Thank you, Deb.

Terry Steele and Arthur Morris are special friends who happen also to be world-class nature photographers. It is my good fortune that they share their "seconds" with me. What a wonderful resource and inspiration! Thank you both. It's fun seeing the birds through your eyes.

And a final thank-you to the folks at North Light, especially my editor, Kathy Kipp. As a first-time North Light author, there was plenty to learn, and Kathy's patience made it easy. Thanks also to Dawn Korth, Marilyn Daiker and Angela Lennert Wilcox.

Table of Contents

About the Artist

Sherry C. Nelson's career in painting has been shaped by her love of the natural world and its creatures. "Capturing birds with brush and paint, as realistically as possible and placing them in a setting characteristic of their natural habitat holds a special pleasure for me." Sherry has been painting and teaching her wildlife art for 25 years, and has shared her techniques with thousands of students in every single state, and in countries around the world.

Sherry is an accomplished and knowledgeable birder, and shares her love of birds as well as her love of painting with her students. She claims that field study is so addictive that there are many times she could forsake brush for binoculars.

A skilled and patient teacher, Sherry leads her students through the complexities of bird painting with innovative and exciting techniques. She has developed a unique approach to teaching, breaking down the instruction in such a way that anyone can learn quickly and easily. And she now teaches almost entirely on camera, demonstrating her methods step by step on closed-circuit TV, making it possible for her students to master skills and techniques impossible with ordinary demonstrations.

Sherry was born in Illinois and received her B.A. from Southern Illinois University. The lure of the Southwest prompted a move to New Mexico, where her children Neil and Berit were raised. She currently lives and paints on her 37 acres of spectacular wilderness in the Chiricahua Mountains of Southeast Arizona.

Now, from her studio in wooded Cave Creek Canyon, Sherry invites you to join her in painting some of the most beautiful of America's garden birds.

Projects: *Paint 11 Beautiful Birds with Sherry*

1 Black-capped Chickadee and Cherries
- Step by Step to a Perfect Eye
- Eye Shape and Placement

PAGE 28

2 Downy Woodpecker and Tulips
- Creating a Textured Look

PAGE 38

3 American Goldfinch and Daisies
- Varying Flower Colors

PAGE 46

4 Northern Mockingbird and Magnolias
- Songbird Tail Structure

PAGE 56

5 Western Bluebird and Morning Glories
- Making Perfect Feather Lines

PAGE 66

6 Brown Thrasher and Tiger Lilies
- Giving a Painting Pizzazz

PAGE 76

7 Ruby-throated Hummingbird and Fuchsia
- Creating Iridescence

PAGE 84

8 Fledgling Bluebird with Butterfly
- Try a Different Butterfly

PAGE 94

9 Northern Cardinals and Spring Blossoms
- Pay Attention to Details

PAGE 102

10 Bewick's Wren and Johnny-Jump-Ups
- Perfecting Detail Markings

PAGE 112

11 Barn Swallow
- Photography as a Reference

PAGE 120

Index

PAGE 128

Materials

Oil paints are easy to use, and they last forever since you'll use very small amounts of paint for any one painting. You can purchase inexpensive paints, but they contain less pigment and more oil, so you'll end up getting less for your money. Quality paints are a good investment.

Always buy the best brushes you can afford. If you are a beginning painter and you attempt these projects with poor quality brushes, you may blame yourself if your paintings don't turn out right. Using good brushes from the start, anyone can succeed with my method.

If you have painted in oils before, you no doubt have many of the supplies you need. If you have not, begin with just a few of your favorite projects from this book to minimize the expense, but always start with the best materials you can afford.

Basic Supplies

• *Palette Pad*. A 9" x 12" (22.9cm × 30.5cm) disposable strip palette for oils is best.

• *Palette Knife*. A flat painting knife is best for mixing in drier and applying thinned oil paint on backgrounds for antiquing.

• *Oil Paints*. I used a total of twenty colors for all the projects in this book: Titanium White, Ivory Black, Raw Umber, Raw Sienna, Burnt Sienna, Burnt Umber, Prima Gray, Cerulean Blue, Indigo, Prussian Blue, Cadmium Scarlet, Winsor Red, Alizarin Crimson, Permanent Magenta, Purple Madder Alizarin, Yellow Ochre, Cadmium Lemon, Cadmium Yellow Pale, Cadmium Yellow and Sap Green. You may certainly substitute colors from your own stock. Just check them against what I used and make the mixes as close as possible.

• *Cobalt Siccative* (or Cobalt Drier). This product is optional, but I would certainly encourage you to try it. When used as I do, your painting will be dry overnight—yet it leaves the palette workable until you are finished with the painting.

• *Brushes*. Red sable brights (short-bristled flat brushes) in sizes 2, 4, 6 and 8. Red sable round (a skinny, pointed brush), in size 0 or 1, for detailing.

• *Artist's Odorless Thinner* and a tiny capped jar to pour a little into when you paint. I use an empty Carmex lip balm jar—yes, that small!—and I keep it capped until I need it.

• *Masonite Panels* in the sizes suggested for each project. You can purchase large sheets and cut it yourself, as I do, or you can have it cut at the lumberyard. Use the medium-priced ⅛" (.3cm) thick Masonite. Try not to buy the really dark, nearly black

Check the materials for each project before you begin. Purchase supplies you'll need and add to your collection gradually. Always buy the best you can afford. In the long run, quality supplies pay for themselves.

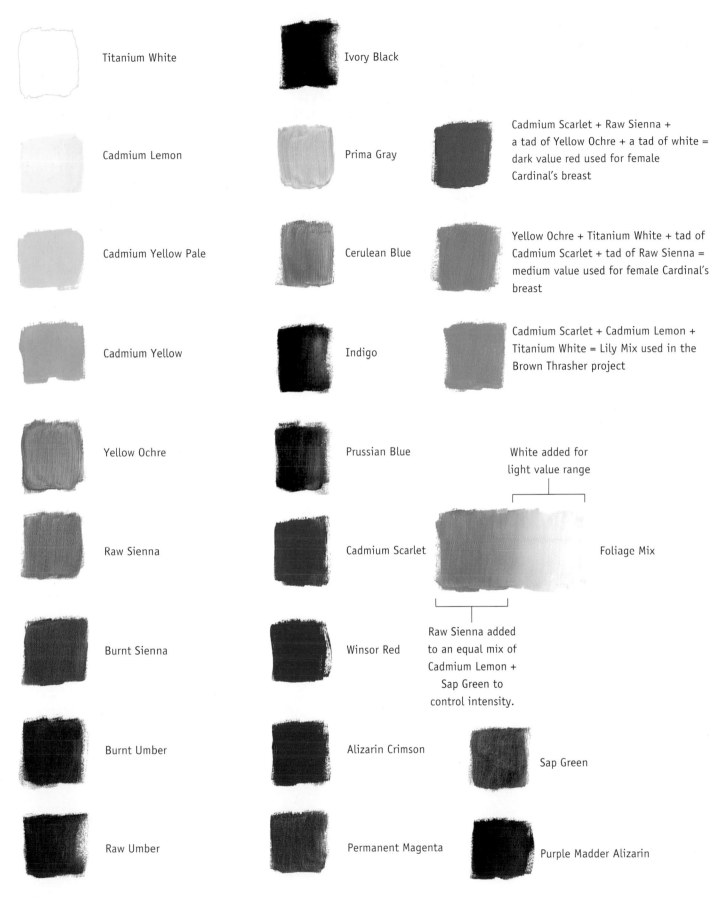

Titanium White

Ivory Black

Cadmium Lemon

Prima Gray

Cadmium Scarlet + Raw Sienna +
a tad of Yellow Ochre + a tad of white =
dark value red used for female
Cardinal's breast

Cadmium Yellow Pale

Cerulean Blue

Yellow Ochre + Titanium White + tad of
Cadmium Scarlet + tad of Raw Sienna =
medium value used for female Cardinal's
breast

Cadmium Yellow

Indigo

Cadmium Scarlet + Cadmium Lemon +
Titanium White = Lily Mix used in the
Brown Thrasher project

Yellow Ochre

Prussian Blue

White added for
light value range

Raw Sienna

Cadmium Scarlet

Foliage Mix

Burnt Sienna

Winsor Red

Raw Sienna added
to an equal mix of
Cadmium Lemon +
Sap Green to
control intensity.

Burnt Umber

Alizarin Crimson

Sap Green

Raw Umber

Permanent Magenta

Purple Madder Alizarin

Oil Colors Used for the Projects

These color samples will help you determine the oil colors you'll need
for each project. Included are swatches of some of the more difficult
mixes so you can get just the right color.

hardboard. It's made more waterproof, and the slicker surface sometimes makes painting difficult.

• *Artist's Graphite Paper* for transferring the design. You'll need a sheet of dark gray and a sheet of white. Buy it at an art supply store in large sheets—not in rolls from a craft store. The craft papers will not work as well and sometimes are not thinner soluble.

• *Tracing Paper*. A 9" x 12" (22.9cm x 30.5cm) pad will work fine.

• *Stylus*. You can use a worn-out ballpoint pen or the end of a brush handle for etching feather lines back into the wet paint.

• *Ballpoint Pen*, not a pencil, for transferring designs.

• *Paper Towels*. Soft and very smooth. Buy the cheap ones for the kitchen; get the really good ones to wipe your brushes. It'll save a lot of wear on those wonderful little brushes.

• *Spray Varnish*. Final finish for the completed paintings.

Materials for Background Preparation

If you've not painted before, you may wish to simplify your background preparation and concentrate on learning the basic painting skills. As you complete more projects, you may find you want to get a bit more colorful and elaborate. When you do, just purchase a few more colors of acrylic.

These are the basics:

• *Masonite Panels*.

• *Sponge Roller*. I apply all my acrylic background paint with 2" (5.1cm) foam rollers. They give a slightly textured, beautifully even surface for painting.

• *Acrylic Paints*. You may purchase one or two neutral colors and add others for specific projects as you like. I used Accent colors, but you could substitute other brands. For the projects in this book, I used Light Mushroom, Off White, April Showers, Wicker, Wild Honey, Soft Blue, Light Stoneware Blue, Stoneware Blue, True Purple, Pine Needle Green, Sage, Green Olive, Roseberry, New Leaf, Peaches n' Cream, English Marmalade and Pueblo Red.

• *220-Grit Wet/Dry Sandpaper*. It's black, and it's available in packs at the hardware store.

• *Krylon Matte Finish*, #1311. A must. This acrylic matte spray will seal the surface of the background lightly, allowing the oil paints to move easily for blending.

• *Newspaper* to protect your work surface.

• *Paper Towels*. These can be less expensive than your painting towels, since you'll need them just for cleanup.

What Sherry Uses

Compare your supplies to those I use and make any substitutions as close as possible for best results.

• *Oil Paint*. Winsor & Newton Artists' Oils. One color, Prima Gray, is from the Martin F. Weber Co. Prima Oil line.

• *Brushes*. Winsor & Newton Series 710 red sable brights, sizes no. 2, 4, 6 and 8. Winsor & Newton Series 740 red sable rounds, sizes 0 and 1.

• *Palette Knife*. I use a custom-made, flat-bladed painting knife styled after Italian painting knives. It is easy to use in mixing and keeps my hand out of the paint.

• *Cobalt Siccative* by Grumbacher.

• *Acrylic Paints*, all by Accent.

• *Spray Finishes*: Krylon Matte Finish, #1311, and Krylon Spray Varnish, #7002, for final picture varnish.

Sometimes supplies may be difficult to find, especially in remote areas. If you have difficulty locating what you need, you may purchase them by mail:

The Magic Brush, Inc.
P.O. Box 530
Portal, AZ 85632
Or call (520)558-2285 to obtain a catalog.

Off White

Light Stoneware Blue

Peaches n' Cream

Light Mushroom

Stoneware Blue

English Marmalade

April Showers

New Leaf

Roseberry

Wicker

Green Olive

Pueblo Red

Wild Honey

Pine Needle Green

True Purple

Soft Blue

Sage

Acrylic Colors Used in the Background Preparation
These samples will help you match the colors of acrylic, all by
Accent, that I used in the preparation of the various backgrounds.

Preparing the Background

The background can make or break the look of the finished art, depending on how well it's prepared. Set up a worktable and have everything you need nearby. You'll do a better job if you don't have to hunt for something as you work.

Did you ever notice the beautiful out-of-focus backgrounds in many bird photos? The bird is in focus and the background, usually foliage with light and dark areas, is soft and hazy and gives special emphasis to the bird. I like that look, so I adapt my background treatments to incorporate it.

A background should stay in the background of the painting. It shouldn't be so complex or so colorful that it overwhelms your subject matter. Simplicity and neutral colors will allow your design to be the focal point. If you find your background getting too gaudy, you probably won't like the finished product.

All the backgrounds used in this book are adaptations of one of the following methods. So don't be intimidated. What's the worst-case scenario? If you hate what you get, don't add the matte spray. Let it dry, sand it lightly, and start all over again! Success is no farther away than the next coat of acrylic.

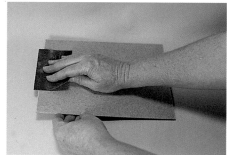

All background preparation begins with sanding. Yes, it's a drag, but it's necessary. With Masonite panels, you don't have to sand the surface to be painted, just the edges. If your panel has a "fuzzy" back, sand that too. I do mine with the electric sander—outside, to keep the grit and dust out of my paint—before I start. Use 220-grit wet/dry black sandpaper. Wipe the sanding dust off with a damp cloth, and you are ready to paint.

Plain Acrylic Background

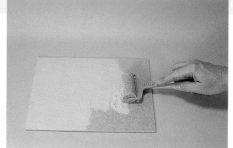

1 The plain acrylic background begins with a single color, equal parts of different colors, or other variations. See, for example, the Chickadee background in Project 1. Drizzle equal parts of April Showers and Wicker acrylic paints onto the surface. How much? If the paint gets bubbly when you roll it, you put on too much. If it disappears into the surface right away, you used too little.

2 Now roll through the paint and spread it around. Roll in one direction until the surface is covered; then go across in the opposite direction for a smoother finish. Lighten the pressure on the roller when you change directions.

Wet-on-Wet Acrylic Background

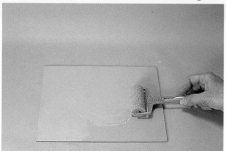

1 Now let's learn the "wet-on-wet" technique. I've used this background method with most of the projects in this book. Begin by sanding the surface and applying a first coat of acrylic in the color specified in the project instructions. Let the first coat dry, then sand lightly, as before. With the same color, apply a second coat. This color is Wild Honey, used for the American Goldfinch and Northern Cardinal projects.

2 Now quickly, while the second coat is wet, drizzle a small amount of a second color, in this case New Leaf, in the center of the surface. Roll into the color lengthwise, not across the stripe.

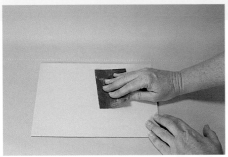

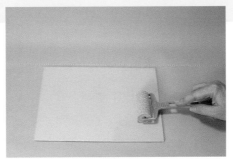

3 After the first coat dries (when it no longer feels cool to the touch) sand it well. Sand the edges again and the painting surface to remove any "cruddies" that may have gotten into the paint. Press lightly with all four fingers on the sandpaper and move it around on the surface as though you were polishing it.

4 Apply the second coat. You'll need a little less paint this time, since the surface has been sealed with the first coat. Again, roll in one direction and then across the other way until the painted surface is smooth and matte.

5 Let the surface dry thoroughly before spraying with Krylon Matte Finish, #1311. Absolutely *always* spray *outside*. I hold the can about a foot from the surface and begin spraying at the top. Working from side to side, I let the spray go off the edge on one side before starting back in order to prevent pileup. I hold the surface to the light so I can see the spray fall, and I move on as I see it begin to coat the surface. You'll soon learn how much is too little (when the oil paint won't blend easily) and how much is too much (when the oils slide too readily).

3 Now begin to move the new color around the surface, changing the direction of the roller every few inches so that the second color becomes splotchy and softened into the wet background. Look closely and you can see that the green does not cover the base coat, but becomes a splotchy accent color softened into the top of it. The colors you use will vary from project to project in this book, but the technique is just the same as you see here. Once the wet-on-wet background is finished, it can be sprayed and used as a painting surface, or further enhanced with oil antiquing.

Final Finish

Not all oil paints dry with an even finish. Some, like the reds and umbers, become dull. Others look wet even when they are dry. To give the surface of a painting a uniform sheen, it is necessary to apply a final finish. Such a finish also protects the paint from becoming damaged or scratched.

When cobalt siccative is used to speed the drying time of your palette, it also shortens the time you must wait before you apply the final varnish. The thickness of the paint you've applied to the painting will also affect the drying time: Obviously, the thicker the paint, the longer you will have to wait for the paint to cure and be safe to varnish. And remember: Just because paint is dry to the touch does not mean it is ready for the final finish.

Since my painting style involves only the thinnest of paint films, and since I live in a warm, dry climate, I can probably varnish sooner than those of you hampered by cold weather and humidity.

Generally, I feel safe varnishing my paintings by the third or fourth week, though I've done it sooner with no problem. I'll leave that decision to you. I use Krylon Spray Varnish, #7002. It is a satin finish, oil-based varnish that gives a very even, light coating and brings out the beautiful rich colors for which oils are noted. I've never had a problem with crazing or other varnish-related problems with this particular product.

Out-of-Focus Oil Antiquing

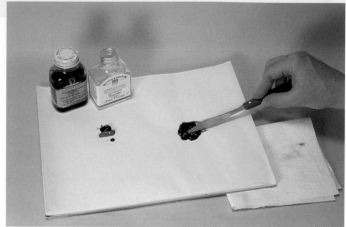

1 Begin the oil antiquing by putting on your palette two small patties of Raw Umber oil paint. Next to one put a slightly larger amount of Sap Green. Touch a drop of cobalt siccative off the tip of the palette knife next to each mix. Then add odorless thinner by dipping the palette knife into the thinner, scooping a little out of the bottle, and dripping it into the mix. About three scoops with the knife should be enough. Then mix the patty of paint, thinner and drier to a creamy consistency.

2 Load a little of the straight Raw Umber mix onto the palette knife. Scrape it onto the painted surface in three or four places. I call these "skritches" because the palette knife "skritches" when you apply the paint thinly to the surface. See how transparent it looks? The trick is not to get too much. Now repeat the process with the Sap Green mix, applying a few skritches randomly on the surface, again, very thinly.

Graduated Acrylic Background

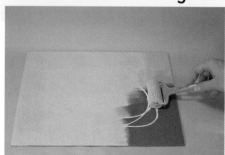

1 The wet-on-wet graduated background is just a bit different and is used for the Mockingbird project. In it we'll place different acrylic colors side by side, creating a value gradation from dark to light across the panel. Begin by basing the surface with April Showers. Let it dry, then sand and re-base with the same color very sparsely.

2 While the second coat is wet, drizzle two inches (5.1cm) of Stoneware Blue in the lower right corner of the surface. With the same roller you used for the April Showers, move the paint around, covering the area.

3 Now drizzle the same amount of Light Stoneware Blue into the center of the surface. Work the roller into it, blending the color into the edges of the Stoneware Blue, creating a value gradation between colors.

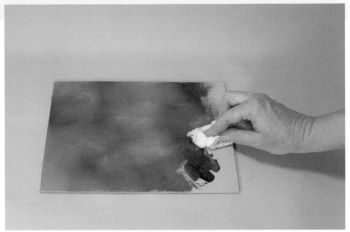

3 Fold a small piece of cotton cheesecloth into a smooth pad. Gently use this to blend the edges of the skritches into the background. Go easy—work around the edge of one at a time, pulling paint gently from the edge out onto the acrylic background. Notice how I've left some space between them at this point. Once all of the skritches have been softened as you see here, open the cheesecloth pad and refold it to expose a clean side.

4 Now, with the dry, clean pad, begin to soften the edges further by joining the splotchy areas together. The goal is to create a value gradation from skritch to background so the antiquing is softened but variegated.

With cobalt siccative in the oil paint, the panel will dry overnight. The next day you can spray it with Krylon Matte Finish, #1311, as you did the plain acrylic panels.

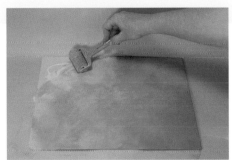

4 In the upper left corner, add a bit of April Showers, and blend this color into the edges of the central Light Stoneware Blue area.

5 One more! Drizzle two inches (5.1cm) of Roseberry on your work surface. Roll through the color lengthwise and blend it a little into the roller. Now go back to the surface and move the roller around some, adding just a touch of the pink here and there to warm the cool blues.

6 When the panel is thoroughly dry, spray it with Krylon Matte Finish #1311.

Transferring the Design

For each of the projects in this book there is a line drawing to make it easier for you to begin painting. Because accuracy is so essential for making your bird paintings realistic, transfer the design from a photocopy of the drawing.

If you cannot make a photocopy of the drawing, you will have to trace it. Work carefully to make your copy as exact as possible, because every variation in the drawing will impact the final appearance of your bird.

Use artist's graphite, sold in large sheets in art supply stores, for transferring. It is important to use graphite that is thinner soluble so you can come back later and clean off the excess graphite. I'll show you how.

1 Lay a piece of dark or light graphite, whichever is specified for the project, on top of the prepared background. Lay the line drawing on top of the graphite and position it as you desire. Tape one edge of the line drawing (not the graphite paper) to the painting surface. Lay a piece of tracing paper on top of the line drawing. Make a tiny mark somewhere on the design and lift the graphite to check that it leaves a mark on the painting surface and not the back of your line drawing.

2 Now you are ready to transfer. Use a ballpoint pen; do not use a pencil, which tends to make wider and less accurate lines as the point wears down. Carefully transfer all detail included in the line drawing. I transfer spots and other pattern areas so that they will show through my sparse base coat later. The tracing paper helps you determine if you have skipped any areas, and it will protect your original line drawing for another use. Check the painting surface after you've drawn a few areas. Is the transfer too light or too dark? Adjust the pressure on the pen to get it just right.

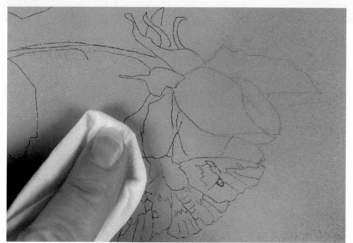

3 On very light backgrounds or when using brand new graphite, the transfer is sometimes too dark. When this happens, fold a dry paper towel into a pad, and use it to rub the transfer firmly. Keep turning the paper towel to a clean side. You can pick up most, and sometimes all, the graphite this way, so be careful not to remove too much. It particularly helps to remove excess graphite in this manner when you are painting a pale flower on a light background—when visible graphite can be hard to control, and white graphite would not work at all.

4 When the design is completed and the paint is dry, you can clean off any excess graphite that still shows around design edges. Dip a large bright (I use a no. 8 because of the firmness of the bristles) into odorless thinner. Blot the brush on a paper towel. Pull the brush along the edge to lift up the graphite line. That is why using graphite that is thinner soluble is important. (A brush dampened with thinner can also be used like an eraser during the painting process. You can lift out small areas of paint, clean up along edges and remove mistakes entirely, if need be. Just remember to dip, then blot. If you leave thinner in the brush, it will bleed out into the painting as soon as the brush touches the surface.)

Setting Up the Palette

Not all disposable palettes are equal. I prefer a 9" x 12" (22.9cm x 30.5cm) size: It is easier to work from and takes up less space than the sizes more appropriate for large canvas work. You must make sure the palettes you purchase are oil impervious. If you place your paint out and an hour later find an oil ring around each patty, the palette is *not* impervious to oils and will ruin your paints by soaking all the oil out of them.

You'll also have a choice of waxy or matte surface. Since pulling dry paint out of the loading zones is a hallmark of my method, I prefer the matte surface. It gives me better control over the paint I'm picking up than does the slicker waxy finish.

Do *not* tear off a single sheet to put the paint on. Leave the sheets attached to the palette so the whole thing doesn't slide around while you work. If you must use a single sheet, in a class for example, tape it in a comfortable position on your painting area so you don't have to hold it down while you load your brush.

Fold two or three paper towels in quarters and stack the folded ends under the edge of the palette. That way you'll have a flat surface to dry wipe the brush on, folds to slide the brush under to squeeze dry, and the palette will hold them down so you don't have to handle them all the time or have them in your way. Then, if you are right-handed, put the whole arrangement on your right. These are small details, but taking care of them up front will save lots of time for the real fun!

1 Here's how I like my palette to look: one-quarter inch (.6cm) of paint from the tube of each color I'll be using, laid out around the outer edge of the palette and about two inches (5.1cm) apart. That's so I have room to mix in the cobalt siccative, and room to make my loading zones between and around the different colors.

2 Dip the palette knife into the siccative and bleed the excess on the side of the bottle. Immediately recap the bottle to keep it from drying out. Now, with this small amount—less than a drop—of siccative on the knife, tap the knifepoint *next* to each patty of paint. The spot of siccative should be the size of a freckle, no more. If your palette is waxy surfaced, the siccative will bleed out a bit; it won't on a matte surface. Use only this tiny amount and *no more*. You want the palette to stay workable for many hours and yet, with the sparse amounts of paint we apply, have the painting dry overnight.

3 Now mix in the drier. Work it into the paint thoroughly, right away, before it dries on the palette. Notice how, after I'm finished mixing it in, I scrape the paint up into a tight pile. That leaves less surface area exposed to drying and extends the life of your palette even further.

How to Keep Your Palette Fresh

If you must stop painting for a while, cover your palette to reduce exposure to air. Since siccative is an oxidizer (drying the paint on contact with the air), the more airtight you can keep your palette, the longer it will last. A palette keeper with a tight fitting plastic lid for the 9" x 12" (22.9cm x 30.5cm) palette is something you may want to invest in.

If you cannot finish your painting within a day or two, simply toss the old paint and put out fresh, since the drier eventually makes the palette unworkable. If you store the palette in a palette keeper and do not use drier in your paint, the paint will last indefinitely.

Loading the Brush and Mixing Colors

A painting surface has a certain amount of tooth and will hold just a small amount of paint stuck down on that surface. Any excess paint you apply on the surface over that slides around easily, mixing with other colors and making what painters refer to as *mud*. Mud comes from getting too much paint on the brush and transferring it too heavily to the surface.

Birds are very detailed creatures. If you apply the base coat color too thickly, all the wonderful surface detail, like feather lines and detail markings that distinguish the bird, will blend into the base coat and disappear. Painting realistic birds and butterflies in oils means learning to paint dryly, with small amounts of paint, so you have maximum control over the detail that you place on top. You'll notice in the photos in this book that I have little if any paint visible on the brush. I load one side only, and I load only a small amount of paint. Dry paint on a dry brush results in good control.

The best way to control the amount of paint you pick up is by loading your brush from *loading zones*.

1 This is what a loading zone looks like. I am using a no. 6 bright and have pulled a little smidgen of paint from the main patty down into a strip of color and worked it into the palette. You can tell there's very little paint there, because the edges of the loading zone are very fuzzy. Once the paint is sparsely and evenly distributed in the strip, I will slip the brush between folds of the paper towel to dry it off. Now the brush is ready to load in the Ivory Black loading zone. You can usually pick up enough paint from a dry loading zone for eight or ten applications of color before you have to pull a little paint down from the patty to feed the zone. But don't add more paint until you just can't get any more paint off the brush onto the painting surface.

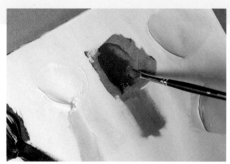

5 Now you have this white brush and want to change colors to a new, completely different mix. Do not wash the brush, but instead clean out the white with a little of the next color you intend to pick up. Here I'm working a bit of Raw Sienna into the brush at the edge of the paint pile, not making a loading zone. Wipe the Raw Sienna out of the brush, taking the white with it, and you are ready to work into the Raw Sienna loading zone, pick up color or make a new mix.

6 Nearly always I make my mixes by working from loading zone to loading zone. But sometimes it's easier to go off to another part of the palette to create a color range that you will be using repeatedly. The Foliage Mix that I use for almost all the greenery in my paintings is an example. Begin by picking up equal-sized dabs of Sap Green and Cadmium Lemon and mixing them into a fat loading zone. Work the colors together in the loading zone so they are thoroughly mixed.

7 Now begin to add Raw Sienna, in about the same amount as you began with the other colors, to the mix. The Raw Sienna will cut the brightness or intensity of the greens and make them more usable in your painting. Keep blending the color in until the green is a subdued, controlled color.

2 Here I'm making a second loading zone of Raw Umber in preparation for making the first mix. It's made the same way as in Step 1. Squeeze the brush dry to remove the excess paint after you've made the loading zone. Now pull the brush through the Raw Umber zone, then through the Ivory Black zone, back to the Raw Umber and back to the Ivory Black. Now you've made a mix of Ivory Black + Raw Umber. If you desire a browner mix, simply load last in the Raw Umber loading zone. If it's a black you're looking for, load last in the Ivory Black. Whichever color you load last will be the majority color on the brush.

3 Let's say we've based the Chickadee's tail in the dark mix. Now we're ready to add detailed feather lines, or in some cases, just a highlight. Slide the brush (which is now dirty) between folds of the paper towel and squeeze gently, wiping out excess paint. With this dirty brush, let's make a white loading zone. Pull the paint out the same as before (see, you're already good at this!) into a dry, "dirty white" loading zone and work the color until it is evenly distributed throughout the strip. This grayed white makes a perfect first highlight that you would not want as bright as the final highlights, and it is also a nice subdued value for feather lines. Many details on your birds will come from this kind of mix, made with white plus whatever color mix was on the brush.

4 When you are ready for final highlighting, squeeze the brush to remove excess paint and make a new loading zone to the side of the old one. This time, since you had dirty white on the brush instead of the dark mix, the white zone stays much whiter for a good strong highlight. White is a very heavy opaque color. Be sure you pull the bare minimum into the loading zone so you keep control of how much you pick up.

8 Wipe the flat brush with which you've been making the mix between folds of the paper towel. Pick up a little dab of white on the end of the brush and make a white loading zone beside the green mix. Pull the paint until it's evenly distributed, and then begin to gradually "walk" over into the edge of the greens with successive strokes of the brush. Then walk back into the white. I go back and forth between the edge of the green and the white stripe several times, pulling the full width of the loading zone each time, until I begin to get a value gradation, from the darker greens to the lighter ones to the lightest area.

This Foliage Mix is nothing more than a controlled-intensity range of green values. I use the darkest values for the initial light-value base coat on my leaves, the middle range of values for my first highlights, and of course, the lightest values for my lightest leaf and foliage highlights. Because greens can muddy so easily, it's worth the time to make this sort of value range from which to load your brush. It will help give you consistent greens rather than muddy ones.

A Dirty Brush?

It's so unusual for me to wash the paint out of a brush that when it's necessary, the instructions in the projects will say so. Washing a brush takes out all the little bits of dirty color, which is what helps you tone and control the intensities in your painting. If you used clean color on the brush at every step, you would have a much more difficult time keeping those strong colors subdued. Keep the lid on the thinner and your flat brushes out of it for the most part. We'll use thinner to make the paint more workable for some detailing, usually with the round brushes.

Sherry's Painting Basics

Before beginning to paint, organize your work area. Put out your palette and folded paper towels (see page 17). Pour a very tiny amount of odorless thinner, no more than ¼" (.6cm) deep, into a small container. Put the cap on the container after each use. If you have purchased new brushes, you may rinse them in the thinner before using. They are packaged with a glue sizing in them, so they will be stiff. Wet them, work the bristles between your fingers until the sizing is softened, and wipe dry on the paper towel.

When you have finished painting for the day, wash brushes first in the dirty thinner that you used while painting and then with clean thinner to remove the last of the paint. You may wish to use an optional brush cleaner in addition. Winsor & Newton makes an Artgel that is an excellent cleaner and conditioner for oil brushes, and there are other brands as well. Find one that works for you and use it. A beautiful new brush with a perfect chisel edge is the key to good bird painting and deserves the best of care.

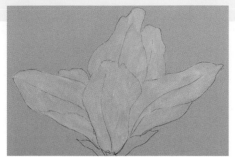

1 This blossom has been based with a sparse, dry mix of Raw Sienna + Titanium White. I pulled the dry loading zones of paint from each of the two colors and loaded the brush back and forth between them as I showed you on page 19. This flower looks a bit yellowish; load last in the Raw Sienna. You can still see graphite lines and background showing through. That's OK. We want a sparse base coat, so when we add other colors for depth and detailing it doesn't get muddy. Notice also the random direction of the strokes.

4 Here's a variation of the approach. The red areas of the tulip have been based just like before, as have the white areas. But the colors in this case meet in a patterned streaking typical of this flower. Here I used the chisel edge to meet the two colors, rather than the flat of the brush.

5 Here's a last example of basing: a branch. The dark shadow color is Raw Umber; the top color is dirty brush (remember, that means it will have a little of the Raw Umber on it) + white. The colors are placed on the branch next to each other, but dry and with a broken edge, just as in the other examples.

6 There are several ways we can blend colors together with the bright brushes. Here's the first: using the chisel of the brush to blend the leaf. Leaves have a natural pattern. Side veins flow into the center vein at an angle, giving the leaf shape and form. To develop that shape with our paints, we can blend from the edge of the leaf toward the center vein with the chisel, the skinny side of the flat brush. Pull the strokes very close together, one after another. Wipe the brush dry every few strokes. If you are lifting paint—scraping it off the surface with the brush—you are holding the brush up too high. Lower the angle of the handle to the surface. The flatter you hold the brush, the less paint you will disturb.

2 Here's an example of another base coat. This is a mixture of Ivory Black + Sap Green applied to the darkest value area of a leaf. Notice again the random direction of the brush strokes and especially how dry and fuzzy the edges of the color look. When you are basing with more than one mix, they have to blend where they meet to create value gradations. Having the edge fuzzy and broken will help the next color meld into it, making your job easier. Do not lay base coats on with hard lines for edges.

3 Here's a cherry based with three different colors: The dark value is Purple Madder Alizarin, the medium value around the edge and next to the dark is Winsor Red, and the light value is Cadmium Scarlet. Look at the sparseness of the base coat: You can still see scruffy holes in the paint. Also notice how the edges of every color are broken, fuzzy and ready to be blended softly into the next color.

7 Cherries have a different construction, so they are blended differently. Lay the flat of the brush on the line where two values meet. Make short, random crisscross strokes along that line. That movement will mix the colors, creating a new value. Do not blend everywhere—just at the junction where two colors meet.

8 Because we want to keep the streaky look that is typical of this tulip, we will blend it in yet another way. Hold the chisel low to the surface and tap it in a line, walking the edge of the light color into the dark and vice versa. Don't pull the brush like you did for the leaf; it will blur the edges of the streaking, which we want defined but softened. Walking with the chisel—tapping the brush—is an effective way to soften two very different color areas without losing the sharp colors. Keep the brush parallel to the growth direction while working each area, so the lines you make while blending follow the natural coloration of each petal area.

9 Branches are also blended with the chisel edge, held parallel to the length of the branch. Make little choppy strokes, touching the dry-wiped brush into the white, then bouncing it down into the dark, carrying a little white texture with it. Now you've picked up a little dark; chop it back up into the light. Keep moving from the light to the dark and from the dark to the light, making a textured surface with the little brush marks. You can think of this as a "chisel-edge chop" or a "choppy chisel." The idea is to set textured brush marks into the surface, giving a realistic look to the branch.

10 Now let's go back to the original based flower. In order to give it shape and form, it has to have dark values that recede from the eye and light ones that come forward. We'll start with darks. This is a little Purple Madder Alizarin, which I have loaded from a very dry loading zone. I have pressured small areas of this color into the natural shadow areas and crevices of the petals, following the natural vein structure. Then I use the chisel edge to blend on the line where the dark value meets the base coat, gradually coaxing the darks to follow the growth direction of the flower. It's important to blend just where the dark meets the base coat—not all over the dark area. You will want to keep a darker dark, an area that you do not blend, to increase the sense of depth in the petal.

11 Now let's apply the first highlight. We'll use a dry-wiped brush in a clean white loading zone. Press on small areas of light in the parts of the petal you wish to accentuate. Do not outline a petal all the way around; light does not illuminate an object that evenly. Use *very* dry white from the driest part of the loading zone, loaded sparingly on the bright, and apply with pressure. Do not use more paint and less pressure, even though when you look at this you might think I've used a lot of paint. And as you apply the white, begin to think about covering your graphite lines.

12 I like to apply all the whites to all the petals at one time; it helps me plan the overall look of the blossom better. With light applied we can begin blending, again on the line where the light meets the base coat, with the chisel held parallel to the growth direction. Walk the brush, pull it softly, tap it from light to base and from base coat back onto the edge of the light, gradually creating a new value between the two areas of color. When all the initial lights have been placed and blended, you can rehighlight with even whiter white in a couple of places to build those final highlights.

13 Subtle highlights can be placed on the tulip in the same way. A lower value white has been pressed on a couple of edges we want to accent. Now use the same technique again: Blend on the line where the colors meet, holding the chisel parallel to the growth direction. Walk, pull and tap the brush to create the transition between the two color areas.

Basic Bird-Painting Techniques

My students call these "bird parts." Some of these terms may seem difficult or confusing at first. But if you learn a couple of new ones each time you paint, they'll soon come naturally. When you find the term "primaries" in the project instructions, just look at this chart if you are unsure about the part to paint. It's so much easier than referring to "that little gray area above the black area on the wing."

And there's a bonus: While observing a bird, I find I can make mental notes on color and texture more accurately because I am familiar with the parts and how they go together.

The various project paintings will feature many special aspects of painting particular bird species. Some techniques will be used only once or twice—and they will be found in the step-by-step instructions. But there are some general techniques—I call them "Bird Basics"—that will help get you started regardless of the projects you choose.

Parts of a Bird

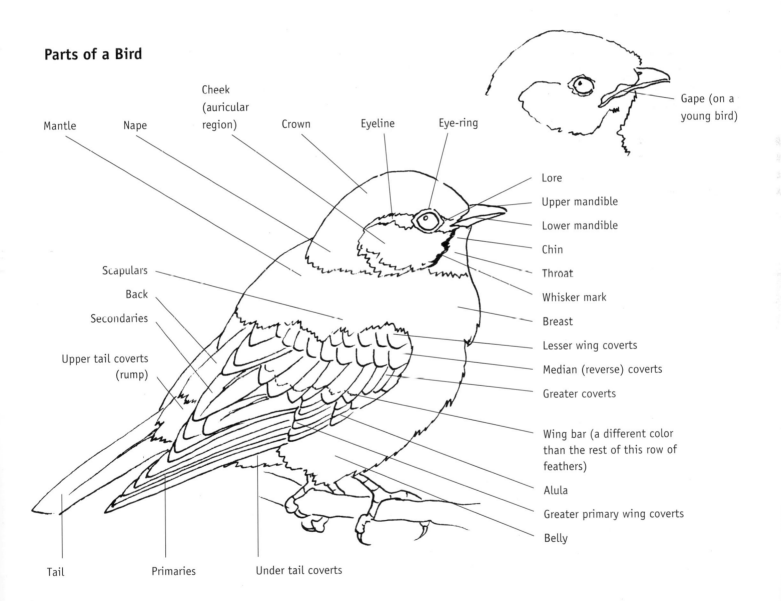

Mantle · Nape · Cheek (auricular region) · Crown · Eyeline · Eye-ring · Gape (on a young bird)

Lore · Upper mandible · Lower mandible · Chin · Throat · Whisker mark · Breast · Lesser wing coverts · Median (reverse) coverts · Greater coverts · Wing bar (a different color than the rest of this row of feathers) · Alula · Greater primary wing coverts · Belly

Scapulars · Back · Secondaries · Upper tail coverts (rump)

Tail · Primaries · Under tail coverts

Head

1 Since the bird's feathers lie in a certain direction, I've found if I base the areas with that direction from the start, it will make my job easier. Here I'm laying the dark base coat on the Chickadee's head. It's solid rather than sparse, because I will add no other colors, and I won't be blending to fill holes. Notice that I'm holding the brush parallel to the growth direction on the cheek, pulling the little zigzag feather marks exactly as shown on the diagram above. When I base the crown, I'll work the brush around the curve, again following the lay of the feathers as shown in the diagram.

2 Now I've filled in the cheek with dry white and will connect the two areas of color with short, feathery strokes of the small bright. I'm using the chisel, pulling tiny strokes just on the line where the dark meets the light. Feathers are short here; don't make long strokes. Work carefully with control. Black and white make gray, but they can easily make mud. Take your time, think about feathery fluff, and use the tiny chisel to make it happen.

Feather Growth Direction

Your painting will look more realistic if you make sure all brush marks follow the natural lay of the feathers as shown here.

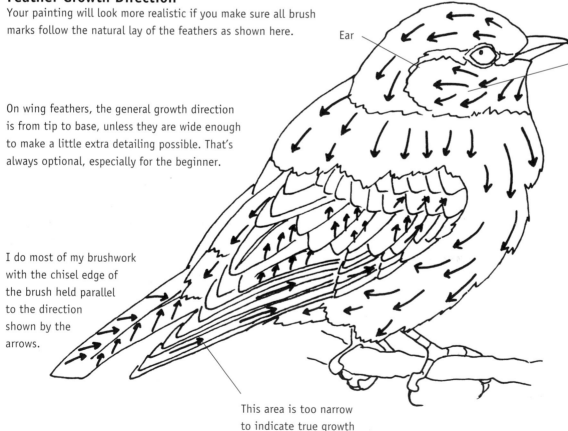

Ear

On wing feathers, the general growth direction is from tip to base, unless they are wide enough to make a little extra detailing possible. That's always optional, especially for the beginner.

I do most of my brushwork with the chisel edge of the brush held parallel to the direction shown by the arrows.

The soft body feathers of a bird have a particular growth direction. You'll find it referred to in every lesson. It's pretty much what you would expect, except for here on the cheek. These feathers sweep back over the bird's ear, protecting it and, in some species, even transmitting sound to it.

This area is too narrow to indicate true growth direction.

Body

3 Body areas on a bird are fluffy and soft. Because I want to duplicate that look, I'll apply my base coat with the chisel, using short strokes and chopping a bit at the surface as I apply the paint, all the while holding the brush parallel to the lay of the feathering in that area. Here the base coat is Raw Sienna + Titanium White, which are loaded from the same dry loading zones as for other elements. I'll load last in the Raw Sienna for darker shadow areas and last in the Titanium White when I'm chopping in areas that will eventually be highlighted. Notice the little choppy chisel brush marks: On birds I call them "tracks," and I like to see them in the paint. They tell the story of the texture in those areas. When I say "leave the brush tracks," this is what I mean. Put them in with choppy strokes and don't blend them out again.

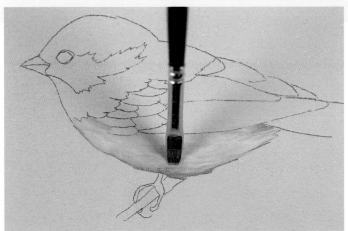

4 Shading is added for contour. Press small amounts of dry paint from the correct loading zone into those areas you want darker. Dry wipe the brush; then blend, using chopping strokes and following the direction of growth, getting a value change between the dark and the base coat.

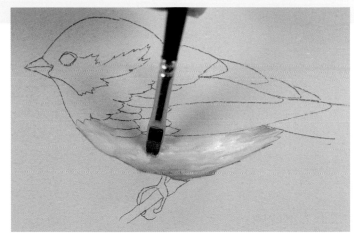

5 Highlight with clean white from a dry loading zone. Use pressure and small amounts of paint. Then blend with a dry-wiped brush. Chop that chisel! Make those tracks, and don't feel compelled to blend them smooth. Think fluff.

Wing and Tail Feathers

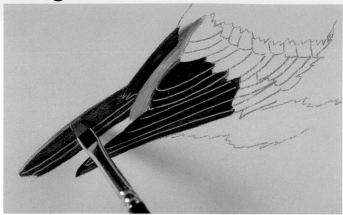

6 Wing feathers are a different matter entirely. They are the firm, stiffer flight feathers that have to be strong to propel the bird's weight and to control in-flight direction changes. As a result, we paint them differently.

I've based (or blocked in) the long tail feathers and the primary wing feathers here. As I block over each line with base coat color, I draw it back into the wet paint. Use a brush handle, an old ballpoint pen, or the finest point of a stylus to etch the feather pattern back into the wet paint. By doing it as you cover the lines, you won't lose track of the placement.

Feather lines require the chisel edge of a bright. The more perfect the chisel on your brush, the better. And the less paint you load, the better. Make a very dry, dirty white loading zone. Squeeze the brush very dry between paper towel folds to remove paint and to reshape the chisel. Hold the brush very flat to the palette surface and pull lightly through the driest part of the loading zone. There will be hardly any paint on the brush, which makes it just right. After making the feather line, reload exactly the same way—every time.

Now look at the position in which I'm holding the brush. I want to start the line at the tip of the feather and slide upward. I have placed my brush so I am working to the outside edge of the feather, holding the brush at a 45° angle to the surface. Lift the brush gradually as you reach the end of the line, just like an airplane lifting off the runway.

Right! Placing the brush at a 45 degree angle to the surface produces a perfect feather line. Load the flat side of the brush in a very dry loading zone.

Never hold the chisel vertically for feather lines and never use a liner brush. Short-bristled red sable brights blend the feather line in.

Beak and Markings

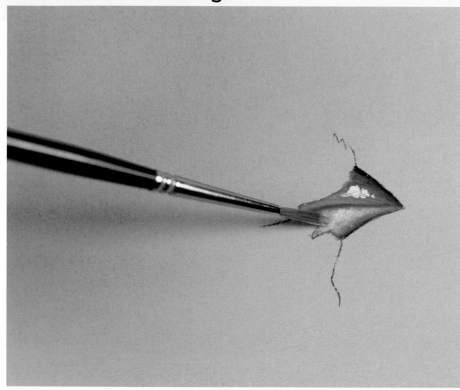

9 When oil paints are applied with a flat brush, they lie flat and do not reflect much light. But if you dab on a little excess paint, and then tap around in it, it stands up in little peaks. Then the flat look becomes strikingly reflective. This method is called *stippling*.

Here the beak is based and shaded and looks pretty dull under the highlight. Poke the point of the round brush into the patty (not the loading zone) of white paint. Put a few gloppy dabs in the middle of the areas you want highlighted. Squeeze the round brush between the folds of the paper towel. Use your fingertips to separate the bristles, flattening them into a scruffy little blender. See how the brush looks flat in the photo? Tap on the line where the dabs meet the base coat and walk the color outward, away from the strong light. Go back in another area and do it again. Don't touch the center white; leave it for the strongest highlight. The texture really makes the area glow.

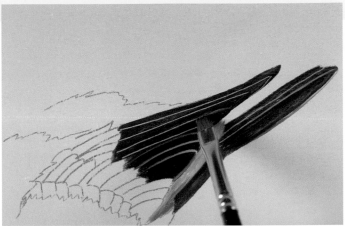

7 Now to pull the other side of the tail feather, I turn my painting surface so that my brush is over the feather and working toward the outside edge. Reload the brush. Starting at the tip, pull to the feather base, lifting gradually. And remember, no one makes perfect feather lines all the time. So what do you do when the line gets fat and messy? Just clean it up with base coat. (See "Making Perfect Feather Lines," page 71.)

8 Feather lines aren't that difficult, but you'll have to practice. Reread all the hints and instructions here and in the individual projects, and you'll get it, I promise. And one more thing: An old scruffy brush won't work, no matter how hard you try. Get a good brush with a perfect edge—and keep it just for feather lines.

10 Spots and other fine detailing on birds are painted with the round brush and thinned paint. Dip a drop or two of thinner from your container and mix a little oil paint into it. It should be quite thin. Now roll the round brush to a point and load into the thinned paint, about halfway up the brush. Make the markings shown here with individual lines, pulled on next to each other so that they join. Make the lines different lengths, so the markings have a natural variation. Remember the three "spot and dot" rules: 1) Vary in size, 2) Vary in spacing between them, and 3) Vary in value. You have to do all three to give a random, realistic feel to the markings on your birds.

Sherry C. Nelson

1 Black-capped Chickadee and Cherries

The tiny Black-capped Chickadee and its close cousin, the Carolina, are found in many areas of the United States and Canada. They are most often thought of as winter visitors, since they come so readily to a snow-covered feeder for their favored sunflower seeds. But you could find these perky birds in your garden cherry tree in midsummer too. The sight of one of these winged acrobats clinging upside down in search of a snack will elicit a smile and cheer up the dreariest day.

Materials

To paint the background, you'll need:
- Hardboard (Masonite) panel, 14" x 11" (35.6cm x 27.9cm), ⅛" (.3cm) thick
- Sponge roller
- Acrylic paints (by Accent)
  April Showers
  Wicker
- Paper towels
- Protected work surface
- 220-grit wet/dry sandpaper
- Krylon Matte Finish, #1311

To paint the Chickadee and Cherries, you'll need:
- Oil paints
  Ivory Black
  Titanium White
  Raw Umber
  Raw Sienna
  Winsor Red
  Cadmium Scarlet
  Cadmium Lemon
  Purple Madder Alizarin
  Sap Green
- Brushes
  nos. 2, 4 and 6 red sable brights
  no. 0 red sable round
- Odorless thinner
- Cobalt siccative (optional)
- Palette knife
- Paper towels
- Disposable palette for oils
- Dark graphite paper
- Tracing paper
- Ballpoint pen
- Stylus

PHOTO BY DEBORAH A. GALLOWAY

Chickadees can be incredibly tame. This Black-capped was begging for a handout from the author at Morton National Wildlife Refuge in New York. Morton claims "the world's friendliest Chickadees"; I believe it!

Black-capped Chickadee and Cherries

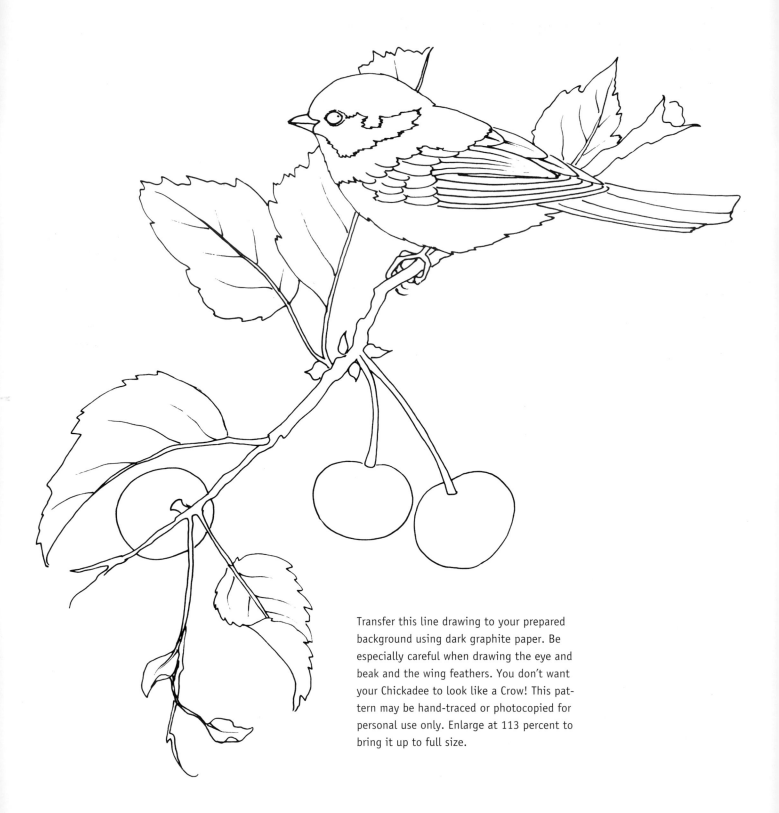

Transfer this line drawing to your prepared background using dark graphite paper. Be especially careful when drawing the eye and beak and the wing feathers. You don't want your Chickadee to look like a Crow! This pattern may be hand-traced or photocopied for personal use only. Enlarge at 113 percent to bring it up to full size.

Field Sketches

Adjust a line or two. Add a bit of color. You can easily change my drawing of the Black-capped Chickadee to the species that frequents your feeder.

All Chickadees have one thing in common: a consuming appreciation of sunflower seeds!

A Chestnut-backed Chickadee has wonderful color on its back and flank. It is found in the coastal areas of the Northwest.

The Mountain Chickadee, common to most western states, can be identified by its white eyebrow.

The Carolina is the southern cousin of the Black-capped. From the southeastern United States, it has more evenly gray wings, with less white on the secondaries than the Black-capped.

Begin with Tail and Primary Feathers

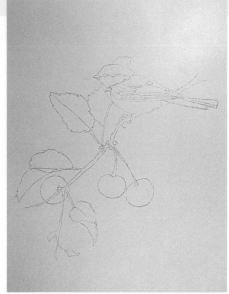

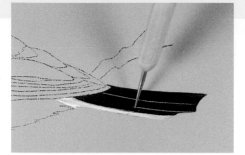

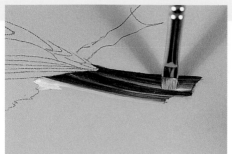

To paint this Chickadee, first prepare a 14" x 11" (35.6cm x 27.9cm) Masonite panel with an equal mix of April Showers and Wicker acrylic paints (both made by Accent). Let dry, then spray lightly with Krylon Matte Finish before transferring the drawing.

1 Base the dark areas of the tail with a mix of Ivory Black and Raw Umber. Remember, you'll make most color mixes with your brush, loading back and forth between the colors, pulling color from dry loading zones. As you paint over the graphite feather lines, mark them back in with a stylus—quick, before you forget where they are. When all the dark areas are based, wipe your brush on a paper towel and make a white loading zone. Then pick up dry white and finish basing the rest of the tail.

2 With some dirty white on the same brush, highlight a bit at the end of each dark feather. Soften this color back into the feather. Then, with fresh dry dirty white on a no. 6 bright, slide in feather lines on top of the ones you drew with the stylus. Always start at the outer tip of the feather and pull back, lifting the brush gradually as you near the end of each line. Add a few extra streaks on the dark feathers, as well as where the dark meet the light, to make the feathers look more realistic.

Paint Highlights and Wing Coverts

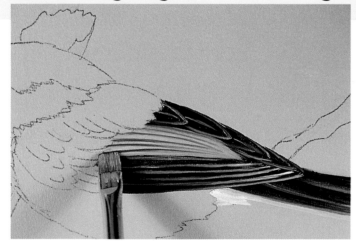

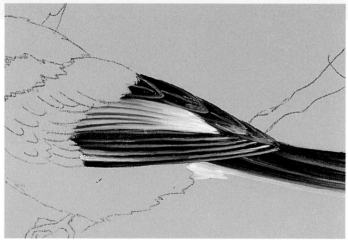

5 Load your no. 6 bright brush with a dark mix of Ivory Black and Raw Umber. Pull dark feather lines, using the brush's chisel edge on the white area. Start at the base of these feathers with each stroke, and always reload in the dry loading zone for every feather line.

6 With a bit of cleaner white, highlight at the tips of the white feathers, softening back into the feathers. It's OK if some of the dark lines are softened while doing this.

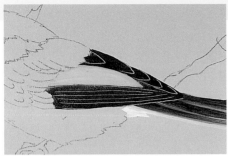 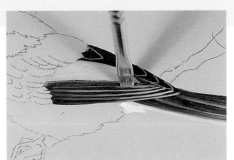 

3 Using the same dark mix, fill in the long primary feathers on the near wing, as well as the tips of the primaries on the far wing. Be sure to draw in the lines with the stylus as you go, keeping the shapes as accurate as possible. Wipe your brush well, then load in with Titanium White. Fill in the rest of the wing area, again drawing in stylus lines to replace covered feather lines.

4 Load your no. 6 bright brush with dry white. Streak in light feather lines on dark areas, beginning at the outer tip of the feather and sliding toward the base. Lift your brush gradually so the feather edge doesn't end too abruptly. Pull shorter lines, one on each side of the feather tip, on the far wing. Use a no. 4 bright and a darker value of white for these. Curving the lines slightly makes the feather look more realistic.

 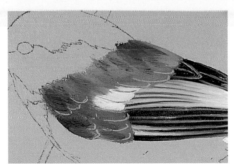 

7 The wing coverts are mostly based in a gray mix of Ivory Black + Raw Umber + Titanium White. Make the mix a middle value, not too dark and not too light. As you fill in the covert area with this mix, mark in the small feather tips with the stylus. Fill in the small area above the white wing feathers with white.

8 Using a mix of Ivory Black and Raw Umber loaded on your no. 4 bright, apply some dark shading areas. Soften these into the base coat using choppy strokes and following the natural growth direction of the feathers.

9 Wipe the no. 4 bright and load into dirty white. Lay each feather line on top of the stylus lines you marked in. If they seem too light, just add more of the dark mix to your white loading zone.

Add Breast Feathers and the Eye

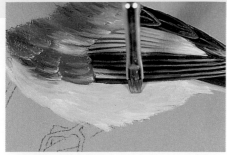 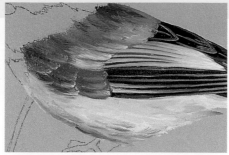 

10 Base the breast and belly area with a mixture of Raw Sienna and Titanium White. Use dry paint and chop the colors on with the brush's chisel edge. Follow the natural growth direction and let surface texture begin to develop, even at this early stage. A no. 4 bright will leave the right size tracks for this area.

11 Now load the no. 4 bright with the dark mix, quite dry, and begin shading color along the edge of the breast and belly. Use choppy strokes, leave texture tracks, and make sure they all follow the direction of growth.

12 Using a no. 0 round brush, make a light gray mix. Fill in the narrow eye-ring with this color. Wash out the brush and touch the tip into the mound of black paint. Use this to fill in the eye shape, aligning carefully with the beak. Don't get it too big—or too small! Check the size against the line drawing as you work. When it's just right, wipe the black out of the round brush, touch the tip into pure white paint and add a highlight dot.

Step by Step to a Perfect Eye

1. Start with the eye-ring. Use a round brush to outline around graphite line of eye with Raw Umber + Titanium White. Thin a bit if needed.

2. Rinse brush in thinner, and fill in eye with Ivory Black. Remember to shape and align correctly.

3. Base top of head and around eye with Raw Umber + Ivory Black, using a no. 4 bright.

4. Cover up even more of the eye-ring. Make it narrower in front than in back.

5. Narrow down the eye-ring one more time, until it's just a hairline's width in front. Add highlight dot.

13 Base in the rest of the head and beak, using Ivory Black and Raw Umber for the dark areas and Titanium White for the light. Follow the line drawing carefully, using the no. 4 bright to edge the darks and lights together where they meet. Narrow down the gray eye-ring by covering it up with the dark mix above the eye and in front of the eye.

14 Using the no. 4 bright, make the final feathery connections between the dark and white areas. Do not blend them together, but rather allow a little of the dark mix to track over into the white and vice versa, making sure texture follows growth direction. Finish the eye area by narrowing the eye-ring in front of and above the eye to just a hairline. Allow it to remain slightly wider at the back of the eye and blend it into the white cheek below the eye. Highlight the beak with a little dirty white.

Eye Shape and Placement

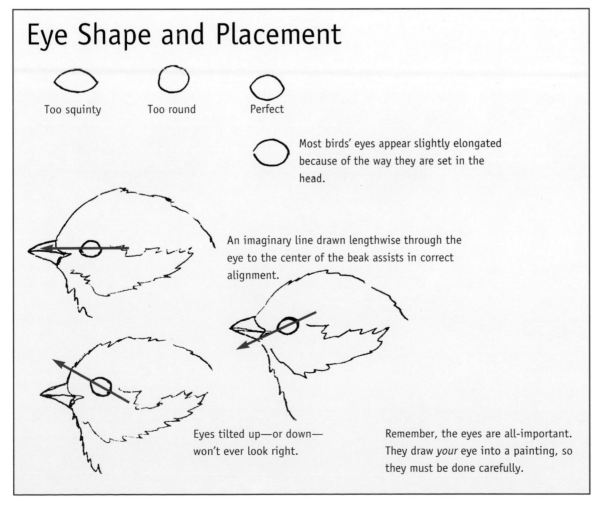

Too squinty   Too round   Perfect

Most birds' eyes appear slightly elongated because of the way they are set in the head.

An imaginary line drawn lengthwise through the eye to the center of the beak assists in correct alignment.

Eyes tilted up—or down— won't ever look right.

Remember, the eyes are all-important. They draw *your* eye into a painting, so they must be done carefully.

Paint the Bird's Foot, the Cherries and the Leaves

15 Base the toes and remainder of the foot with a dark mix of Ivory Black and Raw Umber. Use a no. 2 bright for this step, and keep paint dry on the brush. Then highlight the nearest two toes with a bit of dry dirty white, blending slightly with the flat of the brush.

16 Dip the no. 0 round brush into a little odorless thinner and then into the dark loading zone. Wipe the brush dry, then load a bit of the thinned mix onto the tip. Place fine, slightly curved segment lines on the bird's foot, about ⅛" (.3cm) apart. Add dark toenails using the point of the brush.

20 The leaves are blocked in with two different values of green, using the same mixes as for the cherry stems. Use a no. 6 bright and pull paint into the loading zones for each color, keeping them dry. Apply the dark value first with Sap Green + Ivory Black. Wipe the brush, then mix a light value green, as shown in foliage mixes on pages 18 and 19, with equal parts of Raw Sienna, Cadmium Lemon and Sap Green, plus a bit of Titanium White to lighten. Apply this around the dark value. Break the lines where colors meet so they blend easily.

Blend with the chisel edge, making strokes very close together to form a surface growth direction. If your lines get too busy or too heavy, hold the brush more parallel to the surface while blending.

Base the bottom two-thirds of the branch with Raw Umber. Base the top third with a dirty brush plus white.

21 Add a little more white to the light green leaf mix from lighter values of the foliage mix, and place a few highlights on the leaf edges. Dry brush, then blend with the chisel edge as before, softening the effect by holding the brush low to the painting surface.

Add the central vein and side veins with the same light green and the chisel edge of the brush. Start the main vein at the top of the leaf, but start the side veins at the central vein, pulling outward. Finish the branch by using choppy strokes with the chisel edge held parallel to the length of the branch.

17 The cherries are based with three values of red: The dark area is Purple Madder Alizarin, the medium is Winsor Red and the light is Cadmium Scarlet. Keep the colors dry in their respective loading zones and begin with the dark value first, wiping the brush before applying the next value.

For the cherry stems use two values of greens. The dark value is a mixture of Ivory Black + Sap Green. The light value, shown in the foliage mixes on pages 18 and 19, is an equal mix of Raw Sienna + Cadmium Lemon + Sap Green with just a touch of Titanium White to lighten the value. Use a no. 4 bright to base the cherries and the stems.

18 Using the same brush, begin softening the dark value and the medium value together, blending where the colors meet and working one cherry at a time. Then wipe the brush and blend between the medium and light values on each cherry. Use a choppy brush motion and, to create a sense of roundness, work around the cherry rather than up and down or across it.

When all the cherries are blended, wipe the brush and blend the stems, tapping the chisel edge along the stem where the dark and light values meet. Your goal is to create a new, third value by mixing a bit of the dark and light where those colors join.

19 Highlights must be built gradually so they don't muddy. Load a bit of dry Cadmium Scarlet + dry Cadmium Lemon onto the no. 4 bright. Lay a stroke of this color on each cherry, forming a small square. Wipe the brush off, then blend around the edges of the mix, softening some of the color into the base coat. Wipe the brush well, then load a mix of Cadmium Lemon + Titanium White onto the brush and make a smaller square of this color on top of the previous stroke. Wipe the brush and blend around the edges of the stroke. Leave a little bit unblended. With a little of the same light mix, add other small highlights if desired.

Highlight the stems with a mix of Cadmium Lemon + Titanium White. Place a little of this mix in the middle of the original light value area and soften it with a tapping motion of the brush, walking up and down the stem. Rehighlight with more of the same mix if desired, using slightly more white for a stronger spark.

Now your Chickadee is just about complete. Paint the final details, referring to the finished painting on page 28.

Sherry C. Nelson

② Downy Woodpecker and Tulips

The little Downy is the smallest of the twenty-two different kinds of Woodpeckers in North America. They're frequently found at feeders in every state except Hawaii, and because they are so tame and unwary, they are great fun to observe. Put out some sunflower seeds and invite a Downy to visit!

Materials

To paint the background, you'll need:
- Hardboard (Masonite) panel, 14" x 11" (35.6cm x 27.9cm), ⅛" (.3cm) thick
- Sponge roller
- Acrylic paints (by Accent)
  April Showers
  Pueblo Red
- Paper towels
- Protected work surface
- 220-grit wet/dry sandpaper
- Krylon Matte Finish, #1311

To paint the Downy Woodpecker and tulips, you'll need:
- Oil Paints
  Ivory Black
  Titanium White
  Raw Umber
  Raw Sienna
  Sap Green
  Alizarin Crimson
  Winsor Red
- Brushes
  nos. 2, 4 and 6 red sable brights
  no. 0 red sable round
- Odorless thinner
- Cobalt siccative (optional)
- Palette knife
- Paper towels
- Disposable palette for oils
- Dark graphite paper
- Tracing paper
- Ballpoint pen

PHOTO BY DEBORAH A. GALLOWAY

You spot this Woodpecker drumming. Quick, look at the bill-to-head ratio! Is it a Downy?

Downy Woodpecker and Tulips

Transfer this line drawing to your prepared background using dark graphite paper. Be especially careful when transferring all the little lines on the head, eye and beak. Remember, the better the transfer, the better the painting! This pattern may be hand-traced or photocopied for personal use only. Enlarge at 125 percent to bring it up to full size.

Field Sketches

ACORN WOODPECKER

Sitting at my painting table, I watch these clowns, four or five at a time, tussling over the peanut feeder just outside. Rowdy, rambunctious and noisy.

DOWNY WOODPECKER

HAIRY WOODPECKER

From a distance, with nothing to compare to, the smaller Downy can be confused with the similar Hairy. To distinguish the two species, look at the size of the beak and compare it to the head size. The little Downy's beak is half its head length; the Hairy's beak is proportionately much larger.

Begin with Breast and Belly Feathers

You will need a prepared Masonite panel, size 14" x 11" (35.6cm x 27.9cm) for the Downy Woodpecker. Base the panel, using a sponge roller, with April Showers. Let dry. Rebase, and while wet, use the same sponge roller to soften in a drizzle of Pueblo Red. Work red around the edges and upper portion of the panel. Let dry, then spray with Krylon Matte Finish.

1 Base the belly with Raw Sienna + Titanium White, making the mix slightly whiter as you reach the top of the area where the throat will connect. Try to save the spots by not covering them too heavily. That will give you a guide for their placement later. Base the wing with a mix of Ivory Black and Raw Umber.

2 At both the left and right sides of the belly, shade with a little Raw Umber. Soften the color into the base coat, following the growth direction. Highlight with Titanium White at the top of the area. Add three or four feather lines on the wing with dirty white, using the chisel edge of the no. 4 bright brush.

Paint the Throat and Eye

5 Base throat with Titanium White. Add a bit of shading at the top, under the chin, with Raw Umber. Add a bit more at the left side, just above the markings. Now, with some Titanium White on a no. 4 bright, chop with the growth direction where throat feathers overlap the breast and belly. Work until softly graded light to dark.

6 Base the eye-ring with Raw Umber + Titanium White. Fill in the eye with Ivory Black. Add a highlight dot of Titanium White. Lay in white stripes on the face with Titanium White, using a no. 2 bright. Finally, fill in the area behind the beak with Raw Sienna + Titanium White.

7 Base the small area behind the white eye stripe with a mix of Winsor Red + Alizarin Crimson. Highlight with a tiny bit of Titanium White in the center of the red area. Then fill in the remaining head area with Ivory Black + Raw Umber, using a no. 2 bright and being careful to connect the dark areas to the white with the chisel edge of the brush. Don't blend—you'll get mud!

Fill in the beak with the same mixture, and highlight it a little with your dirty brush plus Titanium White. Then double-check: Is the eyeline narrow enough? Are the connections between the white and dark markings feathery? Retouch if necessary.

4 Base the toes with a mixture of Ivory Black + Raw Umber. Highlight a bit with dirty white in the center of each one. Add thinned Ivory Black toenails with the round brush.

3 Pull out a little Raw Umber and Ivory Black into a patty on the palette and thin with odorless thinner. Using a no. 0 round brush, detail the breast spots, making each spot with a series of short lines.

Creating a Textured Look

Use a no. 4 or no. 6 brush for this size bird.

Apply colors with short "chops" of the chisel edge, following the growth direction. Hold the chisel parallel to feather growth and let the tracks show.

Apply shading and highlight areas with pressure. Apply in the same direction as feather growth.

Using chisel edge, chop and "walk" out the edges of dark and light areas. Leave tracks in the paint. Always follow growth direction with each step.

Most markings are created with a series of lines, just like they lie across the individual fibers on a feather. Use a pointed brush and thin paint.

Create Bark Texture and Tulip Petals

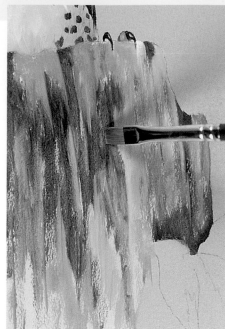

8 The wood is based with three colors: Raw Umber, Raw Sienna and a mix of Raw Umber + Titanium White. Lay on the Raw Umber first, establishing it in the shadow areas and in other streaks as well. Then lay on some Raw Sienna next to each of those areas. Finally, lay on the lightest value, the Raw Umber + Titanium White. You may work the entire tree stump at one time or just do a part.

9 Blend to connect the three values. Use the no. 6 bright or a larger brush, if you wish. Work with the direction of the wood grain, blending and softening until the colors take on a woodlike look.

10 Add detail now, with the chisel edge and straight Raw Umber. Lay on lines and tap on irregular markings to imitate barklike texture. Highlight with the dirty brush plus white on a few of the lightest areas for additional contrast and shape.

Blend Tulips and Finish with Leaves

14 Connect the red areas to the white, using the chisel edge of a no. 4 bright. Work along the line where the colors meet, and try not to pull too much white up or too much red down into the white. Use the chisel to create a central vein line of white in the main petals. Remember to keep the chisel parallel to the growth direction in each area of the petal you are working.

15 Add white highlights on red areas where needed to separate the front petals from the rear ones. Don't let your highlights get lighter than the white based areas. Then blend, using the no. 2 or 4 bright, depending on the size of the petal. Work with the growth direction. And remember, always hold the chisel parallel to the direction the flower grows.

11 Base the light lower portions of the tulip petals with Titanium White. Use the chisel edge to make broken edges where the reds will connect later.

12 Shade at the bottom of the white petals with a bit of Raw Sienna or Raw Umber or Sap Green. Any—or all—can be used to give the necessary depth and shadow in those areas.

13 Fill in the remaining areas of the tulip with a mixture of Winsor Red + Alizarin Crimson. Add a bit of Raw Sienna if needed to keep the reds from being too intense. Vary the proportion of reds in your mix: Use more Alizarin Crimson for darker shadowed petal areas and more Winsor Red for front petals.

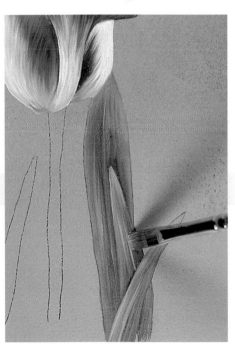

16 Before beginning the leaves, soften the bottom of the tree stump behind the leaf areas. Use a soft, folded paper towel or piece of cheesecloth. The wood should remain more detailed at the top of the stump than at the bottom.

17 Lay dark shadow areas in each leaf using a dark mixture of Ivory Black and Sap Green. Fill in the remaining areas of leaf with a light green mix, made with the dark mix plus Titanium White. If the light mix appears too gray, add a bit of Sap Green to adjust the color.

18 Blend lengthwise down each leaf, holding the chisel low to the surface. When the darks and lights are softened together, add highlights where needed to separate the front leaves from the back. Use the light base coat mix with a bit more white added to it. Finally, add central veining with the light mix using the chisel edge.

③ American Goldfinch and Daisies

One of America's favorite backyard birds, the American Goldfinch is also one of the most easily recognizable in its brilliant summer plumage. But winter brings flocks of paler birds, quieter replicas of their summer cousins, to the feeders. The scientific name is Carduelis tristis. Carduus *is Latin for thistle. A more appropriate name couldn't be found, since the Goldfinches favor thistle seed as a food and delay their nesting until midsummer when they can line their nests with thistledown.*

And who's this munching on sunflower seeds? The wing markings give it away, as does the black cap that's almost there: winter-plumage American Goldfinch.

It's a windy day and a bit hard to focus binoculars or camera. But look at this little male American Goldfinch industriously collecting thistledown to help out at home.

PHOTOS BY DEBORAH A. GALLOWAY

Materials

To paint the background, you'll need:
- Hardboard (Masonite) panel, 18" x 14" (45.7cm x 35.6cm), ⅛" (.3cm) thick
- Sponge roller
- Acrylic paints (by Accent)
  Wild Honey
  New Leaf
- Paper towels
- Protected work surface
- 220-grit wet/dry sandpaper
- Krylon Matte Finish, #1311
- Oil Paints
  Raw Umber
  Sap Green
- Disposable palette for oils
- Palette knife
- Cobalt siccative (optional)
- Cheesecloth
- Odorless thinner

To paint the Goldfinch and daisies, you will need:
- Oil Paints
  Ivory Black
  Titanium White
  Raw Umber
  Prima Gray
  Raw Sienna
  Sap Green
  Cadmium Yellow Pale
  Cadmium Yellow
  Cadmium Lemon
  Winsor Red
- Brushes
  nos. 2, 4, 6 and 8 red sable brights
  no. 0 or 1 red sable round
- Odorless thinner
- Cobalt siccative (optional)
- Palette knife
- Paper towels
- Disposable palette for oil paint
- White graphite paper
- Tracing paper
- Ballpoint pen
- Stylus

American Goldfinch and Daisies

Transfer this line drawing to the prepared surface using white graphite paper. Use a tracing paper overlay to ensure accuracy. Watch the eye, beak and other small details. This pattern may be hand-traced or photo-copied for personal use only. Enlarge at 182 percent to bring it up to full size.

Field Sketches

Many people mistakenly call the Goldfinches "wild Canaries." But the Canary is a songbird native to the Canary Islands and has long been kept as a cage bird.

In Germany, the European Goldfinch is called *Distelfink* which translates to Thistlefinch. That's a perfect name for this thistle-loving bird.

LAWRENCE'S GOLDFINCH
The black face and contrasty yellow and black wings make this I.D. a cinch. But first you have to find one to see; California is the best bet.

Heavy conical beak

Note narrower beak

LESSER GOLDFINCH
You will find these guys doing acrobatics on swaying weed seed heads. They're not much bigger than a minute, but so striking with black crown and green back! I see these southwest birds in winter and summer.

PINE SISKIN
They may seem dull when surrounded by Goldfinches, but get your binoculars focused and check out the lovely touches of yellow on the wings. Pine Siskins are even more widespread than American Goldfinch, and not so contrasty. Young Siskins are very yellow!

Start with Tail and Wing Feathers

This background is painted with Wild Honey and New Leaf using the wet-on-wet technique. Then it's enhanced with oil antiquing using Raw Umber and Sap Green. For a detailed description of how to paint it, see "Preparing the Background," pages 12-13.

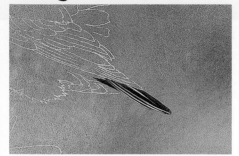

1 Base the Goldfinch's tail with a mixture of Ivory Black + Raw Umber. Quickly draw in the feather lines with the stylus so you don't lose them. Wipe the chisel dry on a paper towel, load it sparsely in a dirty white mixture, and lay in feather lines on the tail to cover the stylus lines. Rotate your painting so the brush is over the tail while pulling the lines, and remember to pull from the tip of the feather to the base.

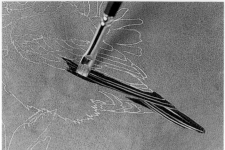

2 Base the primary wing feathers with Ivory Black + Raw Umber. Redraw the lines with your stylus, then add these dirty white feather lines. Use a no. 6 bright with dry paint. Again, work with the piece rotated and begin each feather stroke at the tip of a feather and pull toward the base. Reload your brush with dry dirty white for each and every line.

Paint the Vibrant Breast and Highlights

6 Base the under tail coverts with white. Shade them with a little of the dark Raw Umber + Ivory Black mix. Use the shading to form rough feather shapes. Base the areas of the breast and back, which would be more naturally shadowed, with Cadmium Yellow Pale. Base the rest of the area with Cadmium Lemon. Chop on color with a no. 6 bright, following the growth direction. Use sparse paint; it's OK if it's a little see-through. We'll add more paint later. Base the one visible toe with Raw Sienna + Winsor Red. Highlight down the center with a little dirty white.

7 Shade with Raw Sienna on the back, at the point of the wing and at the edge of the breast. Blend slightly with the direction of growth. Begin to apply the first highlights with a clean brush. Use small amounts of paint and plenty of pressure to set the paint down on the surface. Use Cadmium Lemon + Titanium White. Note the broken, patchy look. Don't get in the bad habit of laying on highlights in spots. Think broken edges.

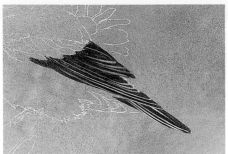

3 Now base the secondaries, stacked on top of the primaries. Use the same mix of Ivory Black and Raw Umber, but this time leave the margin at the edge of each feather open, so when you fill it in with white, it will stay clean. If you get a little messy and get the dark mix where you don't want it, just clean it out with a large bright brush dampened with thinner. Check the next step so you know how wide and how long a margin you need to leave open for the white.

4 Using a clean no. 4 bright, carefully lay in pure white along the edge of each feather where you left the open space. Try not to get it blended into the black below the line. Work with the piece rotated—and remember to pull feather lines from the tip. Since the line can be a little wider, you can use a bit more pressure on the brush than usual. When those are finished, use the same brush to base the bottom wing bar with white.

5 Base the rest of the bottom covert row with Ivory Black + Raw Umber. Base the smaller wing bar above that with white also. Now divide the greater coverts into individual feathers with a few streaks of very dirty white, pulled just like the longer feather lines, but with less paint and pressure.

8 Using a dry brush with little or no paint on it, blend the lights, following the growth direction. You may rehighlight at this point with more of the Cadmium Lemon + Titanium White or even some straight white. But don't worry too much about any transparency. We'll deal with that as the colors begin to dry and will hold strong highlights more easily.

9 Lay in the eye-ring with white, using the round brush. Add the black eye and white highlight dot. Base the yellow on the bird's head with sparse Cadmium Yellow Pale. Remember to follow the growth direction.

10 Narrow the eye-ring as you apply Raw Sienna shading on the yellow areas under the beak and at the back of the head. Detail the area around the eye with a little dotted line of very sparse Raw Umber + Ivory Black. More dark in the corner behind the eye helps define that area too. Highlight the cheek with Cadmium Lemon + Titanium White. Add it twice to get it stronger if you wish; then wait until your painting dries for final lights.

Paint the Beak

11 Base the upper mandible of the beak with Winsor Red + Raw Sienna. Add a little Raw Umber to that mix for the lower mandible. Base the crown with Ivory Black plus a tiny bit of Raw Umber added to speed the drying time of the black.

12 Stipple the beak with a few dabs of white to highlight it. Center the highlight in the fattest part. Dab it in, then wipe the round brush on a paper towel and squeeze the bristles to a flattened tip. Use this to tap around the edges of the highlight to soften it into the base coat. Use less white on the lower mandible so it's not as bright as the upper.

Paint the White Daisies

13 Use a mixture of Ivory Black + Sap Green to block in the dark area on each daisy petal. Use a no. 4 bright, keep the paint sparse, and apply it with the chisel of the brush to stretch it.

14 Fill in the rest of each petal with white. Wipe the brush dry, then blend with the chisel edge.

15 Add more white on the tops of some of the daisy petals to make them lighter, if desired. Then base the centers with Cadmium Yellow Pale + Raw Sienna. Add a little Raw Sienna for shading, stippled on with the round brush and blended with the flattened tip of the round. Then, with a few dabs of Cadmium Yellow Pale, begin to stipple on the first highlight. Dab it on, then flatten the dry tip of the brush and pat the edges of the area to blend it in.

Varying Flower Colors

African Daisy Experiment with different hues to add spark to your next daisy painting.

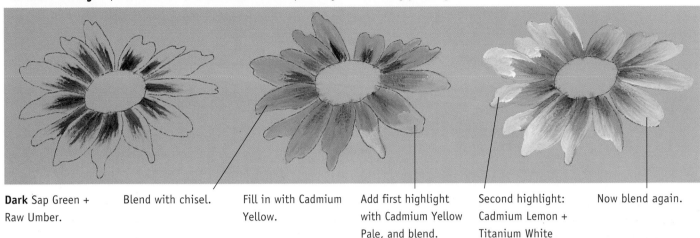

Dark Sap Green + Raw Umber.

Blend with chisel.

Fill in with Cadmium Yellow.

Add first highlight with Cadmium Yellow Pale, and blend.

Second highlight: Cadmium Lemon + Titanium White

Now blend again.

Gloriosa Daisy

Dark Burnt Sienna   **Medium** Cadmium Scarlet   **Highlight** with Cadmium Lemon   **Light** Cadmium Yellow Pale   Blend with chisel.

Painted Daisy
(appropriate name!)

Dark Purple Madder Alizarin

Blend with chisel.

Fill in with white.

Highlight with white.

Blend with chisel.

Centers

Base coat Raw Sienna

Shade Raw Umber

Stipple shading and highlight

Highlight Step 1   Highlight Step 2   Highlight Step 3   Highlight Step 5   Highlight Step 4

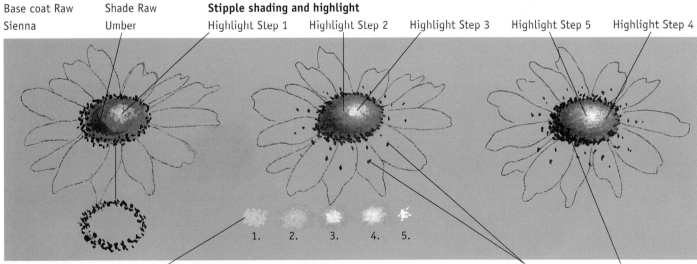

1.   2.   3.   4.   5.

A dot doughnut first, with dots a little wider on bottom left. Wait until the center is done before adding dots.

Stippling steps to build a highlight
1. Dab on Cadmium Yellow Pale.
2. Stipple it out using dry flattened tip of the round brush.

3. Dab on Cadmium Lemon + Titanium White.
4. Stipple it.
5. Dab on a speck of pure white.

Then add a few dots in and around the center.

Thicken and join some dots together on bottom left.

Add Highlights and Details

16 Build highlights on the flower center, getting smaller and smaller in area as you get lighter in value. Use Cadmium Lemon next, dabbing it on, then blending with the flattened tip of the round. Finally, add Cadmium Lemon + Titanium White in a tiny area and blend just enough to create a lovely value gradation.

17 Now add the dots around the daisy center with Raw Umber + Titanium White or with Raw Umber + Ivory Black if you want them more contrasty. The darkest area of the daisy stems should be based with Ivory Black + Sap Green and the lighter center area with a midvalue green from the Foliage Mix you learned to make on pages 18 and 19. Blend the dark and light values where they meet. Then choose a lighter value from the Foliage Mix to highlight down the center of the stem. Soften the highlight just a bit with a dry chisel.

Intensify Color to Finish

20 If you wish, you can intermix yellow African Daisies with the white Shasta Daisies. See "Varying Flower Colors," page 53, to see how to paint them step by step.

21 When the painting is dry, you can come back and add additional sparks of white highlighting on the pickets. Just use the same no. 8 bright, small amounts of pure white, and blend it out as if the other colors were wet. This works perfectly and gives a stronger highlight than you can get when the piece is wet. With cobalt siccative added to your palette, a few hours' drying time is sufficient.

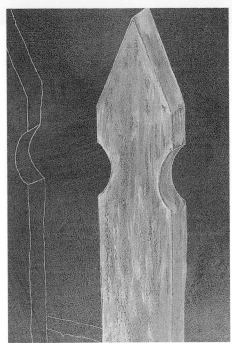

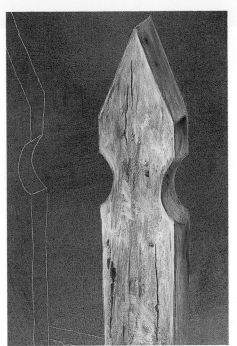

18 Base the white-painted areas of the picket fence with a scruffy sparse coat of Prima Gray. Use the flat side of the no. 8 bright and let the color vary in amount and coverage. Sparsely base the edges of the wood with Raw Sienna + Prima Gray.

19 Add shadow areas with Raw Umber + Raw Sienna, and finally, in the darkest spots, straight Raw Umber. Highlight with white. Add detail with slightly thinned Raw Umber applied with the chisel of the no. 8 bright. Tap the chisel and drag, lifting at times and using pressure at other times to vary the amount of paint that comes off the brush. You'll get more realistic wood grain detail that way. Use a round brush and the same thin Raw Umber to add nail holes or to define the darks further.

22 Increase the strength of color and lightness of highlights on your bird by waiting until the initial painting has dried overnight. Add small amounts of Cadmium Yellow Pale in the darker areas and Cadmium Lemon in the lighter areas. Use a clean brush, small amounts of paint, and chop and blend in the colors exactly as you would if the surface were still wet. Finally, you can build extra lights with Cadmium Lemon + Titanium White.

Now that the head is dry, pick up just a speck of white on a no. 2 bright and add that interesting bit of feathering on the black crown of the bird. The result is lots of interest for very little effort.

Sherry C. Nelson

4 Northern Mockingbird and Magnolias

A common bird in the southern United States, this wonderful songster is expanding its range northward. Often repeated in sets of three or four, the songs are rich and varied and in the spring may continue all night long. They may mimic anything from the neighbor's squeaking gate to the telephone ringing. A Mockingbird is a good parent and will aggressively defend its nest and young. In this painting, I've combined the soft grays of the bird with the pastels of the Chinese Magnolia. Spring is in the air!

Materials

To paint the background, you'll need:
- Hardboard (Masonite) panel, 11" x 14" (27.9cm x 35.6cm), ⅛" (.3cm) thick
- Sponge roller
- Acrylic paints (all by Accent)
  Stoneware Blue
  Light Stoneware Blue
  Roseberry
  April Showers
- Paper towels
- Protected work surface
- 220-grit wet/dry sandpaper
- Krylon Matte Finish, #1311

To paint the Mockingbird and magnolias, you'll need:
- Oil Paints
  Ivory Black
  Titanium White
  Raw Umber
  Raw Sienna
  Sap Green
  Cadmium Lemon
  Purple Madder Alizarin
- Brushes
  nos. 2, 4 and 6 red sable brights
  no. 0 red sable round
- Odorless thinner
- Cobalt siccative (optional)
- Palette knife
- Paper towels
- Disposable palette for oils
- Dark graphite paper
- Tracing paper
- Ballpoint pen
- Stylus

PHOTO BY DEBORAH A. GALLOWAY

Birds don't normally sit still for their portrait! This photo is great for reference—or for another painting. How about this Mocker combined with clusters of blooming dogwood? A stockpile of good photographs is a bird painter's best resource.

Northern Mockingbird and Magnolias

Transfer this line drawing to the prepared surface using dark graphite paper. As always, be very careful when transferring. Do eye and beak and other small details very precisely for best results. This pattern may be hand-traced or photocopied for personal use only. Enlarge at 154 percent to bring it up to full size.

Field Sketches

The family of Mimic Thrushes (*Mimidae*) includes Mockingbirds, Catbirds and Thrashers. All are fine singers and many mimic other birds. The thirty-one species in this family are found entirely in the Western Hemisphere.

BLUE MOCKINGBIRD
(MELANOTIS CAERULESCENS)
Two years ago, my neighbor discovered this striking bird in her yard. A rare visitor from Mexico,
the all-blue Mockingbird showed off for birders
from all over the United States during its
six-week stay here in Arizona.

NORTHERN MOCKINGBIRD
The Latin name, Mimus polyglottos,
means many tongued—and they are!
One Mocker sang eighty-seven different
bird calls without repeating itself!

Begin with Background and Tail

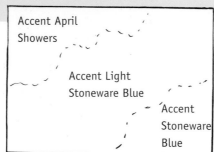

Accent April
Showers

Accent Light
Stoneware Blue

Accent
Stoneware
Blue

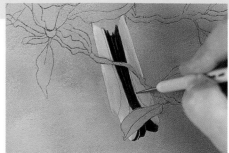

To prepare your Masonite surface, base the panel, using a sponge roller, with April Showers. Allow it to dry. Then, beginning at the bottom right corner of the surface, roll on some Stoneware Blue to cover about one-third of the surface. Next to that, roll on a drizzle of Light Stoneware Blue and blend where the dark value meets the light, using the roller, to get a splotchy effect. Next, roll on enough April Showers to cover the remaining surface, blending into the Light Stoneware Blue area.

This sketch shows the approximate location of the color areas. Squirt a little Roseberry on newspaper or scratch paper and roll into it, picking up just a little. Carry this color to the still-wet background to pink up the surface here and there. Don't add too much. The finished surface should graduate from dark to light from bottom right to upper left, and the colors should be softened together for a splotchy look. Let dry, spray with Krylon Matte Finish, and carefully transfer the drawing.

1 Base the white feathers on the tail with Titanium White. When individual feather lines are covered, draw them back in with the stylus. Base dark areas of the tail with Ivory Black + Raw Umber. As feather lines are covered in this area, draw them back in.

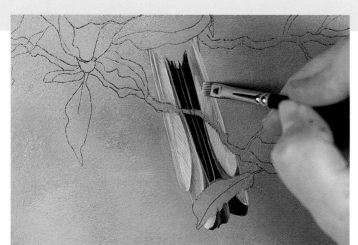

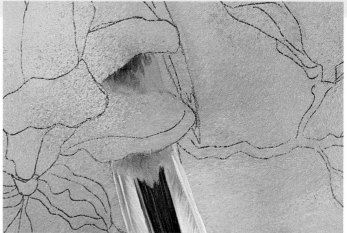

4 Begin blending the white highlights into the base coat. Follow the growth direction using a no. 4 bright and holding it at a 45° angle to the surface. Make individual strokes very close together with the chisel, beginning at the tip of the feather and working toward the base until all the white highlight is softened into the base coat. Do one side of the tail, then repeat the process in the opposite direction on the other side of the tail. (See "Songbird Tail Structure" at right.) While I try to avoid it, you can see in the photo that I'm losing the outline of the branch. When that happens, just clean up the area with a brush dampened with thinner.

5 Base the under tail coverts and lower belly of the bird with a gray mix of Raw Sienna plus a little Raw Umber and Titanium White. Shade at the top of the under tail and at the upper left side of the belly with Raw Umber + Ivory Black. Chop in shading with the chisel to get a textured, feathery surface to the paint.

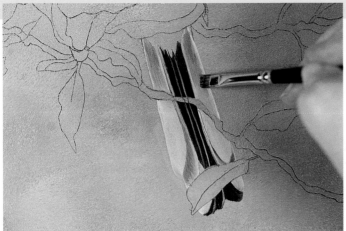
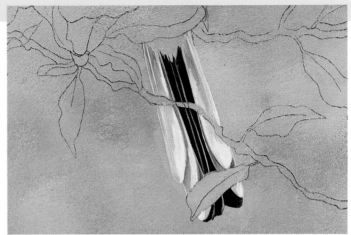

2 At the top of the white feathers, shade with a bit of Ivory Black + Raw Umber. Blend softly with length of feather to fade into the base coat. With a mix of dirty brush plus Titanium White on a no. 6 bright, apply feather lines on top of stylus lines on the dark portion of the tail. Start at the tip of the tail and pull toward the base, allowing the color to fade by the time you reach the end of the line. At the point where the tail intersects the branch, lighten the pressure on your brush to keep from dragging paint into that area.

3 Apply highlights with Titanium White. Use a small amount of paint on the brush, and apply with pressure.

Songbird Tail Structure

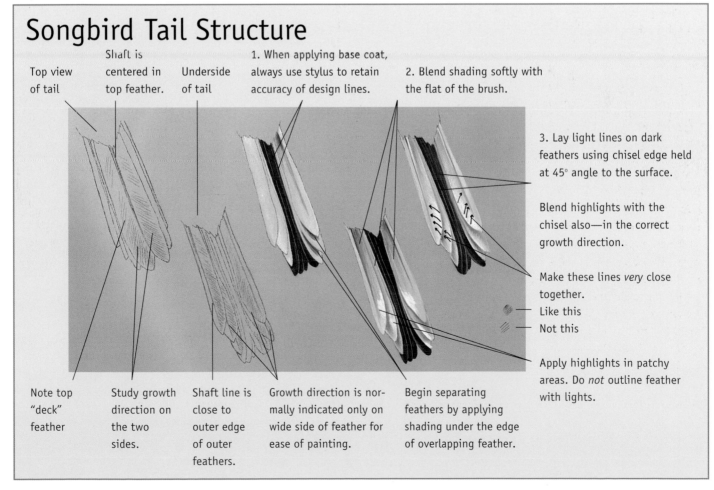

Top view of tail

Shaft is centered in top feather.

Underside of tail

1. When applying base coat, always use stylus to retain accuracy of design lines.

2. Blend shading softly with the flat of the brush.

3. Lay light lines on dark feathers using chisel edge held at 45° angle to the surface.

Blend highlights with the chisel also—in the correct growth direction.

Make these lines *very* close together.
— Like this
— Not this

Apply highlights in patchy areas. Do *not* outline feather with lights.

Note top "deck" feather

Study growth direction on the two sides.

Shaft line is close to outer edge of outer feathers.

Growth direction is normally indicated only on wide side of feather for ease of painting.

Begin separating feathers by applying shading under the edge of overlapping feather.

Paint the Wings

6 Base the primary wing feathers with Ivory Black + Raw Umber. Using the stylus, draw feather lines back into the wet paint as you cover them.

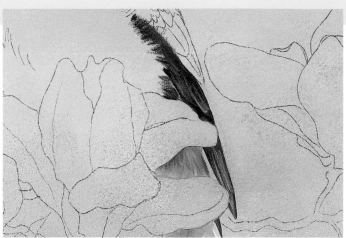

7 Wipe the brush dry, then pick up dirty white on the chisel. Slide the chisel along each of the feather lines marked with the stylus to create the individual feathers. Add a few suggested lines of dirty white to soften primary wing tips.

Create Feather Fluff on the Breast

10 Base the breast of the bird with a mix of Raw Sienna + Titanium White. Chop the colors on roughly using the chisel and following the growth direction. Still using the chisel, pull feather fluff over the edge of the wing to soften.

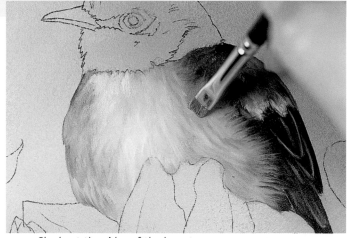

11 Shade at the sides of the breast area using Raw Umber + Ivory Black + Titanium White, mixed to a medium-value gray. Chop in shading and walk the brush out from the sides for texture. Highlight in the central part of the breast by pressuring on white with little paint on the brush. Then, using the chisel, chop where the white meets the base coat. Encourage texture and follow the growth direction.

8 Base the secondary wing feathers with a mixture of Ivory Black + Raw Umber. As the feather lines are covered, use the stylus to draw them back into the wet paint. Base the white tips of the coverts with Titanium White. Base the remaining area of the shoulder with Raw Umber at the top and a mixture of Raw Umber, Raw Sienna and Titanium White at the bottom.

9 With dirty white loaded on the no. 4 bright, apply feather lines on top of those made by the stylus. Using a dry-wiped brush, blend the upper portion of the white tips into the Raw Sienna mix above them. If mixes are too distinct on the shoulder, blend them to soften using the chisel and following the growth direction.

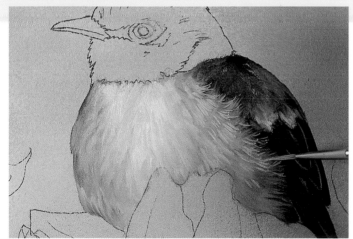

12 For additional detailing on the breast, thin a mix of Raw Sienna + Titanium White, and apply it with a no. 0 round. These fine, feathery shapes will give more realism to the surface than you can get with a flat brush alone. Do not apply too many; a few will have good impact and not be too busy.

Finish with the Eye, Beak and Head

13 Base the eye-ring with Raw Umber + Titanium White, using a no. 0 round. Rinse out the round and dry it on a paper towel. Then use it to base the iris with Raw Sienna + Raw Umber. Rinse and dry the brush again. Finally fill in the pupil with straight Ivory Black. Be very careful to get each of these areas the correct size.

14 Now base between the eye and beak with Ivory Black + Raw Umber. Narrow the eye-ring with this mix in front of the eye until it's nearly nonexistent. Use a mix of Ivory Black + Raw Umber plus a little Titanium White to fill in behind the eye. Use this mix to make the eye-ring at the back of the eye very narrow. Let the two dark areas meet above and below the eye in a narrow band. Allow the eye-ring to show above and below the eye. Outline the iris at the front and back of the eye with Ivory Black, using a no. 0 round. Make this a very fine line, just to define the eye a bit more.

Paint the Chinese Magnolias

18 The Chinese Magnolia is a beautiful blossom that looks harder to paint than it really is. Begin by basing each petal with a mixture of Raw Sienna, Titanium White and a bit of Cadmium Lemon. As the lines between petals are covered, you can draw them back in with a stylus, just like you do feather lines. Then lay in the shadow areas with Purple Madder Alizarin. Load very sparse amounts of color on the brush; then apply with pressure to set the color into the based surface. When you begin blending, do so using the chisel edge parallel to the growth direction in that area of the petal. Tap and walk the edges of the darks until they blend softly into the base coat. Remember that texture is interesting. Don't make your petals too smooth.

19 Load a sparse amount of Titanium White onto the dry no. 4 bright. Then with pressure, apply highlights where indicated. Wipe the brush dry and begin to blend, keeping the brush parallel to the growth direction as you did for the shading color. Tap the brush on the line where the highlight meets the base coat, walking and leading the paint until it softens into the base coat. And remember—not too smooth! Texture in flower petals is realistic and exciting. Don't blend them until they look plastic.

15 Now base the rest of the Mockingbird's head. Use straight Titanium White under the throat and a mix of Ivory Black, Raw Umber and Titanium White on the crown and nape.

16 Shade under the chin with a bit of the crown mix. Highlight the throat with more Titanium White if desired. Shade with Ivory Black + Raw Umber at the nape and forehead, chopping the color into the base coat for texture. Highlight on the crown with some Titanium White, chopping with the growth direction. Use a no. 4 bright for the head; the chisel of a smaller brush will give a texture more appropriate to the smaller feathers of the head. Base the beak, except for the edge of the upper mandible, with Ivory Black + Raw Umber.

17 Fill in the remainder of the beak with dirty white, and blend it into the upper mandible a bit. Add a final highlight on the throat with clean white, applied with the tip of a no. 0 round brush. Stipple the color on in tiny rows.

20 The dark shadow areas on the leaves are based with a mixture of Ivory Black + Sap Green. The remainder of each leaf is based with the dark mix plus a bit of Cadmium Lemon and Titanium White to a soft mossy green. The stems of the magnolia are based with Purple Madder Alizarin + Raw Umber.

21 Set a center vein on each leaf with the light mix. Then blend toward that vein from the edge to the center at an angle that follows the side-vein growth direction. Use the chisel edge of a small bright. Add emphasis if you wish by highlighting in a few places on the leaves with the light green mix plus more Titanium White. Blend the highlighting the same as you did the base coat colors. When the blending is finished, take some of the light mix and redefine the central vein. To finish the branches, highlight with a choppy brush stroke using dirty white. As with the blossoms, texture on the branches is realistic and makes your painting more interesting.

Sherry C. Nelson

5 Western Bluebird and Morning Glories

Birds of open woodlands, farms and orchards, the Bluebirds are among America's most popular birds. Favored nesting sites include tree cavities and fence posts, which are also used by House Sparrows and Starlings. Competition from these introduced species has led to a serious decline in the Bluebird population in recent years. The American Bluebird Association has encouraged folks everywhere to erect specially designed nest boxes and to control their use by other species. The result: a promising comeback of these lovely and valuable birds. Bluebirds (as well as the American Robin) belong to the Thrush family: The heavily spotted breasts of the babies indicate that relationship.

PHOTO BY DEBORAH A. GALLOWAY

A little movement catches your eye, and you focus on this bird. The general build and beak shape indicate it's a Bluebird, as does the blue in the wings. But which one? Look closely at the extent of the rust breast: Can you see that it ends in the same place as on the male in our painting? That and the range are the best field marks. The little female Western Bluebird shown here can be found in most states west of the Great Plains. She would make a wonderful addition to your painting.

Materials

To paint the background you'll need:
- Hardboard (Masonite) panel, 14" x 11" (35.6cm x 27.9cm), ⅛" (.3cm) thick
- Sponge roller
- Acrylic paints (all by Accent)
  Soft Blue
  Stoneware Blue
  April Showers
  Roseberry
- Paper towels
- Protected work surface
- 220-grit wet/dry sandpaper
- Krylon Matte Finish, #1311

To paint the Bluebird and morning glories, you'll need:
- Oil Paints
  Ivory Black
  Titanium White
  Raw Umber
  Raw Sienna
  Burnt Sienna
  Cerulean Blue
  Indigo
  Sap Green
  Cadmium Lemon
  Cadmium Scarlet
- Brushes
  nos. 2, 4 and 6 red sable brights
  no. 0 red sable round
- Odorless thinner
- Cobalt siccative (optional)
- Palette knife
- Paper towels
- Disposable palette for oils
- Dark graphite paper
- Tracing paper
- Ballpoint pen
- Stylus

Western Bluebird and Morning Glories

Transfer this line drawing to the prepared surface, using dark graphite paper. As always, do a very careful job, laying tracing paper over a copy of the original design for best results. Make sure the eye, beak and other details are very accurate for best results in your painting. This pattern may be hand-traced or photo-copied for personal use only. Enlarge at 143 percent to bring it up to full size.

Field Sketches

At some time during the year, a Bluebird can be found in every state—except Alaska and Hawaii—and much of Canada! Southeast Arizona is the westernmost range of the Eastern Bluebird. On our Audubon Christmas counts we tally all three species!

Make the color adjustments (I've given you hints below) and use my line drawing to paint your favorite Bluebird.

All blue in birds is structural color, not pigmented. Individual feather cells refract the light and reflect back only the blue spectrum. Read more on this in Project 7, the Ruby-throated Hummingbird.

MOUNTAIN BLUEBIRD
No rust on the breast. Color is a gorgeous sky blue. Try using Cerulean Blue.

WESTERN BLUEBIRD
Blue of head extends down to meet rust in a line on the upper breast. And blues are so deep in direct light as to have a purple hue.

EASTERN BLUEBIRD
Rusty color extends up under chin. Blue of head and wings is a true royal blue.

Paint Tail and Wing Feathers

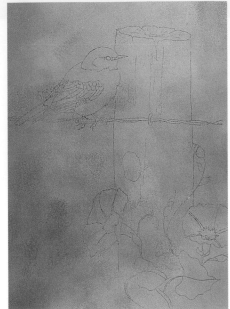

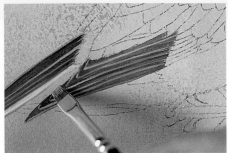

For the background, begin with a coat of April Showers, using a small sponge roller. After it's dry and lightly sanded, recoat the surface with April Showers. While it's still wet, roll in a 2" (5.1cm) drizzle of Stoneware Blue at one end of the panel and a 2" (5.1cm) drizzle of Soft Blue at the other end. Work the colors with the roller until they have softened and blended. Finally drizzle an inch (2.5cm) of Roseberry on your work surface. Soften some of this into the still-wet surface of the panel. Let dry, spray on finish, and transfer the drawing.

1 Base the dark upper part of the tail with a mixture of Indigo and Cerulean Blue. Draw feather lines with a stylus as you cover them. Then lay in feather lines with a mixture of dirty brush plus white, pulling from the tip toward the base of the tail. (See "Making Perfect Feather Lines" at right.) Now work a little clean white into the brush, then wipe it on the paper towel. Reload in a clean white loading zone, and base the outer edge of the tail. Soften the graphite line into the white, letting it act like a bit of shading.

2 Base the primary wing feathers with a mixture of Indigo and Cerulean Blue. Draw stylus lines to indicate feather separations. Wipe a no. 6 bright dry and load into a very dry dirty white loading zone. Lay feather lines over the stylus lines, beginning at the tip of the feather and pulling toward the base. Rotate the panel in order to work *over* the wing. That will lay the sharpest edge to the outside of the feather, where you want it. The short lines indicating the back edge of each feather are optional; you may do them with a no. 2 or no. 4 bright if you wish, using a slightly darker value from the dirty white loading zone.

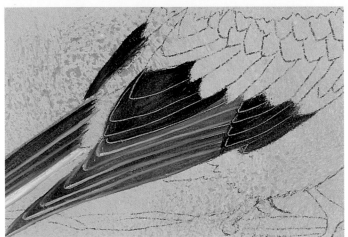

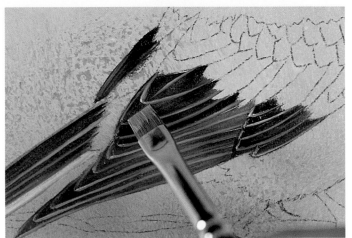

3 Base the secondaries and the greater primary wing coverts with a mixture of Indigo and Ivory Black. Remember to draw in stylus lines as you cover the pattern. It's easy to forget the number and exact location of the lines when the section is completely based.

4 Dry the brush on a paper towel and load it sparingly in your dirty white loading zone. Lay feather lines on top of the stylus lines, pulling from tip to base. If you roll the brush ever so slightly as you make the lines on the secondaries, you will be able to round the feather shape. Remember to turn the panel around to help your brush reach those outer edges. Last, add center shaft lines on the top one or two secondaries.

Making Perfect Feather Lines

Always paint wing from bottom to top.

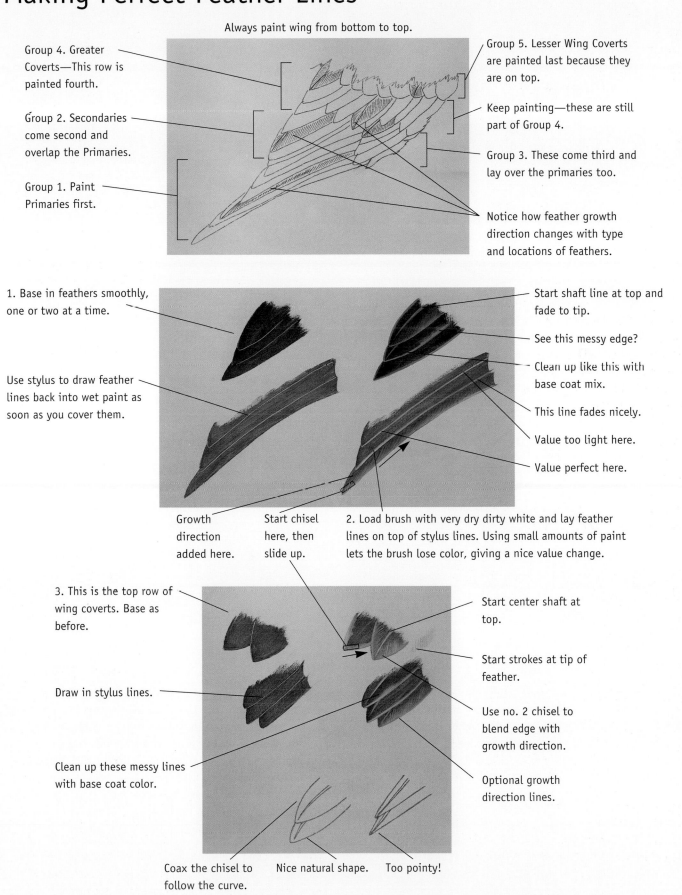

Group 4. Greater Coverts—This row is painted fourth.

Group 2. Secondaries come second and overlap the Primaries.

Group 1. Paint Primaries first.

Group 5. Lesser Wing Coverts are painted last because they are on top.

Keep painting—these are still part of Group 4.

Group 3. These come third and lay over the primaries too.

Notice how feather growth direction changes with type and locations of feathers.

1. Base in feathers smoothly, one or two at a time.

Use stylus to draw feather lines back into wet paint as soon as you cover them.

Start shaft line at top and fade to tip.

See this messy edge?

Clean up like this with base coat mix.

This line fades nicely.

Value too light here.

Value perfect here.

Growth direction added here.

Start chisel here, then slide up.

2. Load brush with very dry dirty white and lay feather lines on top of stylus lines. Using small amounts of paint lets the brush lose color, giving a nice value change.

3. This is the top row of wing coverts. Base as before.

Draw in stylus lines.

Clean up these messy lines with base coat color.

Start center shaft at top.

Start strokes at tip of feather.

Use no. 2 chisel to blend edge with growth direction.

Optional growth direction lines.

Coax the chisel to follow the curve.

Nice natural shape.

Too pointy!

Paint Feather Growth on Wings and Back

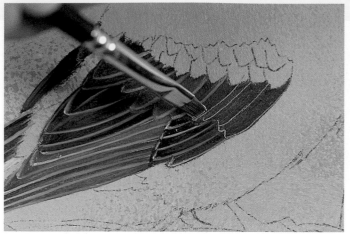

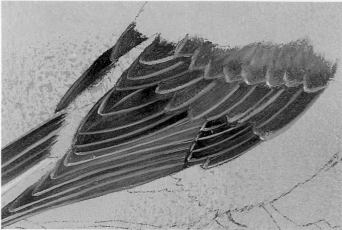

5 Now base the entire next row of feathers with the Indigo + Ivory Black mixture, leaning toward more Indigo. Draw in stylus lines. Replace the stylus lines with a dirty brush plus white, loaded very dry. Note the position of the brush. I'm working from inside the curve of the feather, over the feather to which I'm adding the line. The brush is tilted slightly so the corner away from me is touching down at the tip of the feather. As I start the brush moving upward, I'll roll it *slightly* in my fingers, coaxing the brush to follow the curve of the covert feather. It takes a bit of practice, but when you've mastered it, you'll have perfect feathers every time.

6 Base in last row of feathers with Indigo + Cerulean Blue. Outline them with short, curving feather lines done with dirty white. Use some of the outline to blend up into the feather to set a bit of growth direction.

Add the Breast and Beak

10 Base the under tail coverts with Titanium White and the breast and belly with Raw Sienna. Use the choppy chisel to lay colors in with texture and growth direction.

11 Add accent color on the breast by chopping in short strokes of Burnt Sienna + Cadmium Scarlet. Go easy—this is a strong mix and will quickly make the breast get too red. Add this color in areas outside the ones where you will be placing highlights. Now clean out the brush with a little fresh white. Wipe dry and load it with a little Cadmium Lemon + Titanium White. Then chop in some soft highlights, primarily to the outer edge of the breast. Allow the brush to leave tracks of light over in the dark area for increased depth and texture.

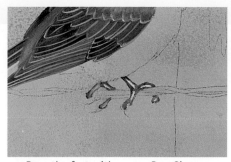

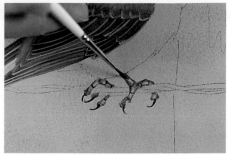

7 Base the back and shoulders of the bird, up to where the head meets the body, with a mixture of mostly Indigo + Ivory Black. Chop in the color for texture with the chisel edge of a no. 6 bright. Follow the growth direction. When the area is blocked in, wipe the brush and pick up dirty brush plus white. Come back and highlight in a few areas, especially above the top of the wing and where the shoulder would round.

8 Base the feet with sparse Raw Sienna + Raw Umber. With a small bright, touch on lines of dirty brush plus white down the center of the shaft of the leg and each toe.

9 Blend the white lines to soften them into the base coat. Thin a little Ivory Black with odorless thinner, and roll the tip of the round brush into the mixture. Apply fine black lines to segment the leg and toes. Add black toenails as well.

12 Base the lower mandible with black. Base the upper mandible with a mixture of Raw Umber + Titanium White. Highlight along the bottom edge with dirty white. Lay in the eye-ring around the eye with Raw Umber + Titanium White using a liner brush. Base the eye with black, and highlight it with a dot of white. Lay in a bit of black between the eye and beak, narrowing the forward portion of the eye-ring as you do so.

13 Base in the remainder of the head with the Indigo + Cerulean Blue mix. If it seems a little bright, add a tad of black to cut the blue. Lay in areas of shadow forms with black at the cheek, nape of neck and below the beak on the chin.

Detail the Eye, Feet and Wood

14 Using a no. 4 bright, begin softening the edges of the black shading, chopping in the growth direction in each area. Remember the growth under the eye sweeps back, not down. When the shadows are softened, add highlights with a dirty brush plus Titanium White. Again, chop on color following the growth direction and using short strokes since the feathers on the head are very small. Lighten areas of highlight by gradually lightening the value of the dirty white mix you use.

15 Base the wire with a mixture of Ivory Black + Titanium White. Shade on the back portions of the wire with black, and highlight the forward curves with white, tapping it on with the chisel edge of the brush.

Create Trumpet-Shaped Morning Glories

18 Base the blue areas of the flower with a sparse mixture of Indigo + Cerulean Blue. Base the separations between the petals with Cadmium Lemon + Titanium White. Base the trumpet with the same yellowish mix.

19 Apply shading at the base of the petals and next to some of the petal divisions using Indigo. Remember to apply shading and highlighting colors using a small amount of paint and lots of pressure on the brush. That will set in the color firmly and help retain good contrast.

20 Using the chisel of the brush, gently connect the shading to the yellow center. Begin to add highlights, pressing them on with small amounts of dirty brush plus white. Add the small areas of Raw Umber and straight Cadmium Lemon in the center of the flower using a no. 2 bright.

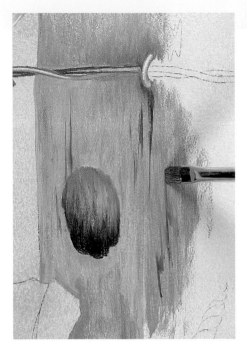

16 The fence post is very gray overall and can be painted entirely with a large bright. Base the darker areas with a mixture of Raw Umber + Ivory Black + Titanium White. Base the lighter areas with Raw Umber + Titanium White. Here and there, warm the color with Raw Sienna. Work all the colors together up and down with the wood grain. Finally, detail the wood graining using Raw Umber. Use varied pressure on the brush, short and long strokes and lines, and even the corner of the brush for a random, realistic look.

17 Add touches of Burnt Sienna below the brad that holds the wire and below some of the small nail holes to suggest rust. Highlight between areas of dark detail with whiter streaks, particularly in the central area of the post.

21 Soften the edges of the white highlights into the petals. Connect the narrow yellow band in the center to the light yellow mix. Finally, soften the edges of the Raw Umber center. Base two or three stamens with Cadmium Lemon. Highlight the tips with white, and shade the base with Raw Umber. Shade the trumpet of the flower with a mixture of Raw Umber + Sap Green.

22 Make a dark green mixture of Ivory Black + Sap Green, and lay in dark areas of leaves and stems. With a bit of the dark on the brush, pull out a little white and Cerulean Blue to make a light greenish mix. Base the light areas of the leaves and stems with this mix. The dark value of the un-opened bud is Cerulean Blue + Indigo. The light areas are the same mix on a dirty brush plus white.

23 Blend the leaves with the direction of growth, using the chisel edge of the larger brush for larger leaves and the smaller brush for the little ones. Add a highlight on an edge or two, and add central veining with the same light leaf mix. Highlight down the stems with the light mix, tapping the color on with the chisel to round the stems. Soften the lines between the dark and light blue on each section of the buds.

Sherry C. Nelson

6 Brown Thrasher and Tiger Lilies

A lovely bird of hedgerows and woodland edges, the Brown Thrasher is not always easy to find. Since they tend to stay low in brush and foliage, sometimes you hear them first. They thrash, using their strong feet to scratch and kick aside twigs and leaf litter to unearth the grubs and other insects, as well as berries, that might make a meal. Observe these birds in dry leaves on the search for dinner and you'll have no doubt how they got their name. The state bird of Georgia, Brown Thrashers may be found along garden edges in most Eastern states. Watch for the bright yellow eye of the adult (gray or brown in a younger bird), and don't forget to listen!

Materials

To paint the background, you'll need:
- Hardboard (Masonite) panel, 14" x 11" (35.6cm x 27.9cm), ⅛" (.3cm) thick
- Sponge roller
- Acrylic paints (all by Accent)
  Light Mushroom
  English Marmalade
  Peaches n' Cream
  Pine Needle Green
- Paper towels
- Protected work surface
- 220-grit wet/dry sandpaper
- Krylon Matte Finish, #1311

To paint the Brown Thrasher and Tiger Lilies, you'll need:
- Oil Paints
  Ivory Black
  Titanium White
  Raw Sienna
  Burnt Sienna
  Raw Umber
  Burnt Umber
  Sap Green
  Cadmium Scarlet
  Cadmium Lemon
- Brushes
  nos. 2, 4, 6 and 8 red sable brights
  no. 0 red sable round
- Odorless thinner
- Cobalt siccative (optional)
- Palette knife
- Paper towels
- Disposable palette for oils
- Dark graphite paper
- Tracing paper
- Ballpoint pen
- Stylus

PHOTO BY DEBORAH A. GALLOWAY

A campsite snapshot, taken so close the whole bird wouldn't fit the frame. It's so easy to lure wildlife in the desert—just offer a little water. Can you tell from my sketches of the Thrashers which one this is? Curve-billed it is. Incredible orange eye!

Brown Thrasher and Tiger Lilies

Transfer this line drawing to your finished surface, using dark graphite paper.
I transfer all the spots and other detail. I find those details will often show
through the sparse paint, remaining as a guideline. And even if the paint covers
it entirely, you will have your tracing paper copy of the pattern to transfer back
onto the wet surface. Take your time—a perfect transfer will pay off in the accuracy of the finished painting. This pattern may be hand-traced or photocopied
for personal use only. Enlarge at 143 percent to bring it up to full size.

Field Sketches

Mockingbirds repeat the phrases of their songs three or more times; thrashers, usually twice; and catbirds, once.

Thrashers sing with enthusiasm from the tallest shrubs in the desert areas. They "thrash" through the dead leaves and scattered twigs, searching for insects, seeds and berries.

CALIFORNIA THRASHER
Found only in California; at 12" (30.5cm), it is the largest of our eight Thrashers.

CURVE-BILLED THRASHER
Found in streamside brush of the southwest. A family nested by the house last year. When I'd drive out, Mom would flatten herself on the nest in the low cholla, keeping her eye on me.

GRAY CATBIRD
Thrashers, Mockingbirds and Catbirds are the three Mimic Thrushes—and what great songsters!

LONG-BILLED THRASHER
Gray on head separates this bird from the similar Brown. Has much the same reddish color as the Brown too, but is found only in southern Texas.

Begin with Tail and Breast

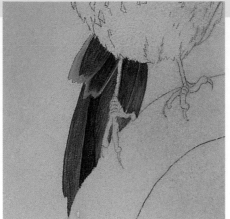

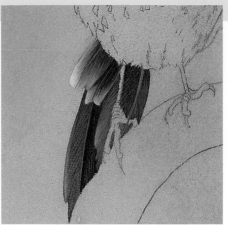

Base then rebase a prepared Masonite surface with Light Mushroom. While wet, drizzle on two inches (5.1cm) of English Marmalade and, in a different area, Peaches n' Cream. Using the sponge roller, move the paint around, softening so the background is slightly splotchy. Drizzle a little Pine Needle Green to add some soft green areas to the bottom of the wet surface. Let dry, spray on finish, and transfer the drawing.

1 Base the darkest long feather and the interior of the top two feathers with Burnt Umber + Raw Umber. Fill in the remainder of the top two feathers with a mixture of Cadmium Scarlet + Cadmium Lemon + Titanium White, a mixture we will use again later and call the Lily Mix. It's a peachy pink. Fill in the half of the feather that's directly behind the bird's leg with Burnt Sienna + Raw Sienna. Base the remaining feather areas of the tail with Burnt Umber + Burnt Sienna.

2 Using a dry brush, blend each half of each feather with the growth direction to establish the fine fiber lines. Add center shaft lines with Raw Sienna + Titanium White. Highlight the tips of the top two feathers with the Lily Mix plus more white and reblend.

Paint the Legs and Features

6 Base the dark areas on the legs with Burnt Umber and the rest of the legs with Burnt Sienna.

7 Burnt Sienna tends to turn pink when white is added. So rather than add the usual light line down the center shaft of the leg and toes for highlighting, I lifted out the light value with a damp brush. Use a no. 4 bright, dip in thinner, blot on a paper towel, and pick up paint, allowing the surface to show through. Soften the line with a dirty brush to blend. Add detail lines and toenails with black, using the round brush.

8 Lay in the iris with Cadmium Lemon plus a bit of Cadmium Scarlet first, using the round brush. Then fill in the pupil with black, and add the highlight dot with white on the line where the pupil and iris join. Outline the yellow iris with black.

3 Base the outer edges of the breast and belly with Raw Sienna and the inner central area with Raw Sienna + Titanium White. Work the colors onto the surface with the growth direction. Use short strokes to suggest the correct feather length. Base with Burnt Sienna + Raw Sienna the little portion of wing showing on the right. Let the spots show through the paint for later reference.

4 Press on several strokes of white in the center of the breast between spots. Use a no. 6 bright and clean white. Blend with short strokes and with the lay of the feathers. Add shading at outer edges of the breast and above the legs with a small amount of Raw Umber + Titanium White.

5 Now begin adding spots, using Burnt Umber in the lighter areas of the breast and Burnt Umber + Ivory Black in the darker shadow areas. Use a round brush, and thin paint slightly if it doesn't go on easily. The spots have a definite shape and are not uniform. Check the line drawing or the original painting frequently.

9 Base the area around the eye with Raw Umber + Titanium White and the throat with white. The forehead can be based with Raw Sienna. Base the rest of the crown and nape with Burnt Sienna. Add a bit of Burnt Umber to the Burnt Sienna for the darker areas at the edges of the head. Walk a little of this reddish mix down onto the neck. Base the beak with Ivory Black + Raw Umber in the darker areas, and add a bit of white to the mix to create the lighter base of the lower mandible.

10 Blend with the growth, using a no. 4 bright, to connect the areas of color you just applied. Soften some of the rusty color into the edges of the gray. Add the small markings with Raw Umber around the eye and on the crown of the bird. Define the spots below the cheek with Burnt Umber + Ivory Black. Highlight on the forehead a bit with small strokes of dirty white. Highlight the upper mandible of the beak with dirty white also.

11 Using the no. 8 bright, rough on the major value areas of the gate. Use Ivory Black + Raw Umber for the darkest values and that mix plus white for the medium values. Keep paint sparse. Notice how you can still see through to the background. Too much paint now makes mud later.

Create Texture on the Gate and Flower

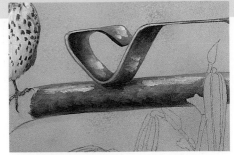

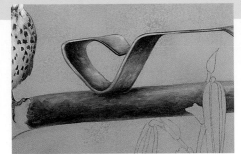

12 Wipe the brush dry, and begin to connect the base coat values. Use the flat of the bright for blending, and make short, crisscross strokes so you don't end up with a distinct pattern. When you've created the new value where the base coat colors meet, you're ready to add the first highlight. Lay it on with a fairly clean white.

13 Soften the edges of the white into the surrounding values. Strengthen the darks with a repeat application of Ivory Black + Raw Umber in places where you may have lost them. Resist the temptation to add more whites. The gate is old and weathered, not shiny—and besides, we don't want it to compete with the bird and lily for interest.

14 The dark value on the lily petals is Burnt Sienna + Cadmium Scarlet. The medium value is the Lily Mix, made with the dirty brush, so it picks up a slightly rusty tone. The light value is the Lily Mix plus more white. Base sparsely and dryly, and if you are careful you can retain most of the spots for later.

18 Base the dark value on the buds with Burnt Sienna + Cadmium Scarlet. Base the rest of the bud with Cadmium Scarlet + Cadmium Lemon + Titanium White (the Lily Mix). Base the dark value on the leaves and stems with Sap Green + Ivory Black. Base the rest of the leaves and stems with a dark value from the Foliage Mix. Always be sparing with applying base coat paint; don't get heavy-handed.

19 Blend the colors with the chisel, softening the values together with the growth direction on both buds and leaves. Highlight the buds with Lily Mix + Titanium White and soften into the surrounding values. Add a few minor veins in the tiny leaves using a light value from the Foliage Mix.

20 Now, for more drama, add a bit of cleaner white to the buds. Blend again—just to soften—into the bud. You can see in the finished painting how the strong lights tie together the bird, lilies and buds and how essential they are to move the eye through the painting.

  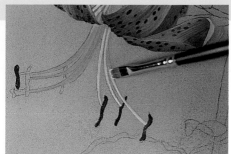

15 Wipe the brush and begin to blend, following the growth direction of each petal and creating fine lines as you work with the chisel. The petals are quite striated, so don't be afraid of surface texture. And the lines give the petal shape and contour, even at this early stage.

16 Lighten the Lily Mix one more time, and add some nearly white highlights. Blend them with the same growth direction. Shade with more Burnt Sienna if an area seems too pale. Add a central dark streak or two on the petals with Burnt Sienna. Finally, add the oval Burnt Umber spots with slightly thinned paint.

17 Base the long stamens with the light-value mix used on the lily. Use your best bright to get nice, clean edges. Add the anthers with slightly thinned Burnt Umber + Burnt Sienna. Add a bit more white to the base mix, and highlight the stamens with a fine line down the center.

Giving a Painting Pizzazz

The elements you choose to include and the way you arrange them can make a painting sing. Let's look at some of the paintings I've done for this book and see how they work.

For years, I've had in mind to combine a Brown Thrasher and a Tiger Lily in a painting. Why? The colors of the bird and the flower are a natural—close in hue and very striking. Tying those colors to a related background helps meld the elements too. But more than anything, it's the spots! The visual impact of the pattern of markings on both bird and flower just seemed so perfect. I think it's a fun, fascinating painting that can't help but intrigue the viewer.

Another example: The light spots on the baby Bluebird quickly pull you to find their match in those on the Blue Flasher butterfly. Color unifies, but the repetition of the attention-getting pattern makes the painting come alive. **A repetitious pattern of spots or other elements can form a visual connection, a bridge, between elements in your painting.**

Another way to give a painting spark is to visually link the elements in order to convey a message or tell a story.

The wren, a garden bird, could certainly be seen on, or nesting in, an old sprinkling can. The Barn Swallow painting subtly suggests the relationship between the old building and the bird's tendency to nest there. **Use your painting to play up interesting connections and to tell a story with your chosen design elements.**

Last, be sure the bird really can be found in the setting in which you place it. The Eastern Bluebird during breeding season can be found in south Texas, home of the Blue Flasher that I chose for added interest. Hummers really do favor fuchsia. And Goldfinches often can be seen feeding on daisy and sunflower seeds. **Match the critter you choose to paint with its habitat. The painting will make more sense and will be naturally more pleasing to the viewer.**

Sherry C. Nelson

7

Ruby-throated Hummingbird and Fuchsia

Materials

To paint the background you will need:
- Hardboard (Masonite) panel, 9" x 12" (22.9cm x 30.5cm), ⅛" (.3cm) thick
- Sponge roller
- Acrylic paints (all by Accent)
  Light Mushroom
  Roseberry
  Off White
- Paper towels
- Protected work surface
- 220-grit wet/dry sandpaper
- Krylon Matte Finish, #1311

To paint the Ruby-throated Hummingbird and fuchsia, you will need:
- Oil Paints
  Ivory Black
  Titanium White
  Raw Umber
  Raw Sienna
  Cadmium Lemon
  Sap Green
  Winsor Red
  Alizarin Crimson
- Brushes
  nos. 2, 4 and 6 red sable brights
  no. 0 red sable round
- Odorless thinner
- Cobalt siccative (optional)
- Palette knife
- Paper towels
- Disposable palette for oils
- Dark graphite paper
- Tracing paper
- Ballpoint pen
- Stylus

"Glittering fragments of rainbows" was how John James Audubon described the first Hummingbirds he saw. Ever since, people have been fascinated with the iridescence of Hummingbirds, their trademark. Equally amazing is their astonishing agility in the air, flying backwards and upside down with equal skill—or hovering motionless before a flower to feed. Fill a feeder with four parts of water to one part sugar, and invite some to your garden or patio. You can't help but be intrigued by these "winged jewels."

The Blue-throated Hummingbird. It's 5" (12.7cm) long—pretty hefty for a Hummer! These guys stay with us all winter. We have videotape of them at the feeder in a snowfall!

The Magnificent Hummingbird at 5¼" (13.3cm) is our biggest Hummer. When light strikes the crown, it glows royal purple. Maintaining feeders is a lot of work, but just look at the rewards!

A Broad-tailed Hummingbird. It's vibrating primary wing feathers make a "zing" when he flies. Look at that throat glow!

PHOTOS BY DEBORAH A. GALLOWAY

Ruby-throated Hummingbird and Fuchsia

Transfer this line drawing to the completed surface, using dark graphite paper. Be especially careful to get the detail exact. Hummers are so tiny, there's not much margin for error. This pattern may be hand-traced or photocopied for personal use only. Enlarge at 125 percent to bring it up to full size.

Field Sketches

With 358 species in the Americas, hummers are the second largest bird family in the world. Hummers' hearts beat 20 or more times per second, and their wings beat 20 to 60 times per second.

Only the Ruby-throat is found regularly in the East, but 15 species of hummers are found west of the Mississippi. Calliope is our smallest hummer—weighing 2.5 grams. A penny weighs 3 grams!

I have 8 kinds at my feeders! In late summer during migration, it's common to see 100 at a time at my window feeders. They drink 5 to 6 quarts of sugar water a day. Big job! Don't bring in feeders in the fall until two to three weeks after you've seen the last bird. They need that nectar when stoking for migration.

NORTH AMERICAN HUMMERS

Broad-billed Hummingbird has red bill, blue throat, green breast.

Black-chinned Hummingbird is the western cousin of the Ruby-throat and has a purple band under the black chin.

Only Hummer in North America with a decurved bill.

Gorgeous guy of the southwest deserts.

Gorget

Rufous Hummingbird, as flashy as a newly minted copper penny, and nests as far north as Alaska.

The Lucifer is found only in western Texas and southeastern Arizona.

Flank

Female Black-chinned on a cold spring morning, fluffed up and sunning herself on the patio.

The Anna's is the only one of our Hummers that has rose pink on crown and throat.

From Tail to Breast, Lay on Color and Texture

Begin by basing the panel with the sponge roller, using Light Mushroom acrylic paint. Let this dry, and rebase. While the second coat is wet, drizzle a little Roseberry onto the surface. Using the same roller, move the pink around and blend lightly into several areas of the surface. Repeat the process, using Off White. Make sure some of the darker value shows through. When the effect pleases you and resembles the panel shown here, let it dry. Spray with Krylon Matte Finish before tracing the design.

1 Base the tail with a mix of Ivory Black and Raw Umber. As graphite lines are covered, draw them back in with the stylus. Then use a no. 4 or no. 6 bright, loaded with dirty white, to lay in the feather lines marked on the tail with the stylus. Begin at the tip of each tail feather and slide the brush upward, allowing the color to fade away at the top of the tail.

2 Base the rump of the bird with a mixture of Sap Green + Raw Umber. Use a no. 2 bright, since this is such a small area.

Add Feet and Begin the Wings

6 Apply Titanium White with the no. 4 bright at the top of the breast and just above the under tail coverts. Even as you apply the color you can begin the process of breaking up the edges, so it doesn't just go on in a spot.

7 Chop and walk the edges of the white highlights to graduate into the base coat. Use the chisel of the brush, as always, parallel to the growth direction. Leave some of the white very clean but still with surface texture. Add feet at this stage, using Ivory Black on the point of the no. 0 round brush.

8 Base the primary wing feathers on both the near and far wing using sparse and dry Raw Umber. Scruff the paint on, stretching it as far as possible.

3 Now add the iridescent markings, using a mixture of Cadmium Lemon + Sap Green loaded on the no. 0 round brush. Thin the paint slightly with odorless thinner if you wish. Make the markings as suggested on the line drawing for this area. See "Creating Iridescence" (page 91) for complete instructions.

4 Base the breast and belly of the Hummer with a pale mix of Raw Sienna, Sap Green and Titanium White. Remember to chop the colors on with the no. 4 bright, following the contour of the bird and the growth direction of the feathers.

5 With the same chopping motion, add a little Sap Green + Raw Umber for shading at the sides of the breast. First press on a bit of the mix, then walk it out, with the chisel parallel to the growth direction. Let the feather texture show some to make it more realistic.

9 With the base coat very dry, it's easy to see the graphite lines underneath. With dirty Titanium White on the brush, begin at the tip of each feather and make the chisel-edge feather lines right on top of each graphite line. Lift the brush gradually, so the line fades as it reaches the upper end of the feather.

10 Working with the chisel edge between the light feather lines at the base of each feather, add a little Raw Umber for shading. Soften the shading into each feather.

Add Iridescent Feather Markings

11 Base the greater coverts with the same sparse Raw Umber you used for the primaries. Lay in dirty white feather lines on top of the graphite lines, again beginning at the tip of each feather.

12 Base the last section of wing, the scapulars, with Sap Green + Raw Umber. Then, with Cadmium Lemon + Sap Green on the round brush, lay in the tiny iridescent feather markings as you did on the rump. Check the line drawing for the size and placement of the markings.

13 Base the eye-ring with Raw Umber + Titanium White. Make it a little whiter and wider at the back of the eye. Then fill in the eye with straight black. Add the highlight dot with white. Then, reshape the eye-ring and narrow it down some as you add the Raw Umber eyeline in front of and behind the eye.

16 Base the gorget with Alizarin Crimson and Winsor Red. At the top of the gorget, just under the beak, shade with a little Ivory Black. Use a stylus to mark the placement and size of the feathers. If you don't like the first arrangement of markings you do, just base over it with the red mix and try again. Having a clear pattern for placement of the iridescent markings will make a big difference in how beautiful they look.

17 Use Winsor Red + Titanium White to lay in all the little feather markings on the gorget. Begin at the bottom of each row and work upward so you lose color off the brush. Use a no. 0 round, rolled to a point, and load it only once for each row. Remember, the colors won't be as bright up under the chin, so don't carry the markings too high. Note the layout of the markings on the line drawing.

14 Base the beak with Ivory Black + Raw Umber. Lay a soft highlight line down the beak, working from the base of the beak toward the tip. Use a chisel edge and dirty white. Hummer beak shapes are hard to keep perfect because they are so narrow. Clean up along the edge with a brush dampened with odorless thinner and blotted on a paper towel.

15 Base the crown of the bird with Sap Green + Raw Umber. Load the Cadmium Lemon + Sap Green mix on the round brush and add the iridescent markings. Check the line drawing for size and placement. Remember, if the paint won't move well, thin it by dipping the point of the round brush into thinner and mixing it into a tiny amount of the green mix. Roll the round brush to bring it to a good point.

Creating Iridescence

Iridescence is a challenge to capture with paint because you are painting reflected light instead of pigment. Iridescence on Hummers is created by the feather structure, not by pigmented color. Light enters the individual feather cell, is broken up, and only the red or green or blue light is reflected back to the observer.

The base of the feather is not iridescent and is covered up by the next feather. Gorget

The chin is in shadow, not reflecting as much light.

Only the feather's tip has color. It's a scallop of tiny lines that lay in a pattern on the gorget.

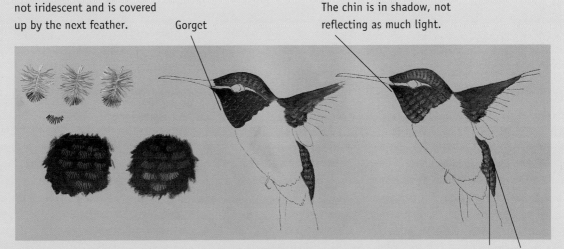

As areas of color are based in, mark feather shapes with a stylus. Note how the shapes follow body contour.

Markings are created with a no. 0 round loaded with a value lighter than the base coat, but in the same color family.

Note how markings don't go all the way to the edge. The dark helps round and contour the area.

Paint the Fuchsia Buds and Leaves

18 Base the left half of each fuchsia bud with a mixture of Alizarin Crimson and Winsor Red. Use the same mix for the right half, but add some Raw Sienna to cut the intensity. Follow the contour and shape of the bud with the chisel to begin to get some realistic growth direction, even at this early stage.

19 Shade the bud on the lower right using Alizarin Crimson + Ivory Black. Highlight on the upper left of the bud using Raw Sienna + Titanium White. Blend the highlight softly into the base coat. With a dry brush, reload into a whiter mix, keeping your second highlight within the first. Finally, lay on some dark lines, even on the light side of the bud, to indicate ridges.

20 Lay in dark shadow areas on the leaves and stems using a dry mixture of Ivory Black + Sap Green. Wipe the brush and add Titanium White to the dark mix, using it to fill in the remainder of the leaves and stems.

Create Soft Texture on the Blossoms

22 Base the red petals of the fuchsia with a mixture of Alizarin Crimson + Winsor Red. Use proportionately more Alizarin Crimson for dark shadow areas and more Winsor Red in the mix for the top or forward petals. Base the light, bottom petals of the flower with Raw Sienna + Titanium White. In darker shadow areas you can add a bit more Raw Sienna to the mix; in areas where the petal will be highlighted later on, you can use a larger proportion of white.

23 Shade the darkest areas of the red petals with a mixture of Alizarin Crimson + Ivory Black. Soften the shading after it is applied with the shape of each petal area. Shade the light petals with very small amounts of Alizarin Crimson, Winsor Red and Raw Sienna. Load from a fuzzy, sparse loading zone. A little will go a long way on the pale background. Blend to soften the shading with a very dry brush. Use the chisel edge to give some suggestion of the surface texture.

24 Now lay on highlights. Use pressure, a dry brush, and very little paint. (Yes, I know it looks like a lot, but it's not!) Highlight the red petals with Cadmium Lemon + Titanium White. Blend, then use straight white. On the light petals, use straight white.

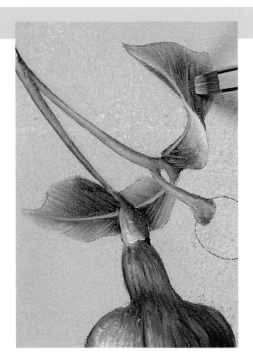

21 Wipe off the brush and begin to blend. Remember to follow the growth direction to establish the shape and form of the leaf or stem you are painting. Pull soft strokes from the edges of leaves toward the center with the brush held very low to the surface and using the chisel. Finish by adding a light center vein.

25 When blending, walk the highlight into other areas of the petal by tapping the chisel edge, like a stutter, from the light toward the base coat. Keep the brush chisel parallel to the growth direction. You may rehighlight once or twice, but don't get the highlights too white. It will be more effective if the sharp whites can play against the darker base coat and shading colors.

26 The stamens are based with the same petal mixes. The top halves are Alizarin Crimson + Winsor Red; the bottom halves, the same mix lightened with white. Base with Raw Sienna + Titanium White. Blend the dark and medium values a bit where they meet, using the dry chisel edge of the brush. Then, with the tip of the round, stipple a bit of white on the end of the stamen to brighten it.

Sherry C Nelson

8

Fledgling Bluebird with Butterfly

All the songbirds I've painted for this book have one thing in common. When they hatched they were blind, helpless and had only a few tufts of down to cover their bodies. They were totally dependent on their parents for the care they needed to survive. But with frequent feedings and the warmth supplied by the parents, they grow quickly. Many songbirds leave the nest, or fledge, at about ten or twelve days of age. This fledgling Bluebird has just left his home for the first time and is beginning to explore the world around him. What fun to share in the adventure through our painting.

Materials

To paint the background you will need:
- Hardboard (Masonite) panel, 9" x 12" (22.9cm x 30.5cm), ⅛" (.3cm) thick
- Sponge roller
- Acrylic paints (all by Accent)
  April Showers
  Wicker
  Soft Blue
  Sage
  Green Olive
- Paper towels
- Protected work surface
- 220-grit wet/dry sandpaper
- Krylon Matte Finish, #1311

To paint the baby Bluebird and butterfly, you'll need:
- Oil paints
  Ivory Black
  Titanium White
  Raw Umber
  Raw Sienna
  Burnt Sienna
  Indigo
  Cerulean Blue
  Winsor Red
  Cadmium Lemon
  Prima Gray
  Cadmium Scarlet
  Cadmium Yellow Pale
  Sap Green
- Brushes
  nos. 2, 4 and 6 red sable brights
  no. 0 red sable round
- Odorless thinner
- Cobalt siccative (optional)
- Palette knife
- Paper towels
- Disposable palette for oils
- Dark graphite paper
- Tracing paper
- Ballpoint pen
- Stylus

PHOTOS BY DEBORAH A. GALLOWAY

Snapshots such as these are a great help when you are looking for ideas for paintings. I like to have a good file of native North American butterfly photos to use with my bird paintings. In recent years, many butterfly houses have opened, such as the one at Callaway Gardens in Atlanta and Butterfly World in Ft. Lauderdale. You are allowed to take your camera through the large screened enclosures. The butterflies are tame and can be photographed on their favored food plants. It's terrific fun and a bonus for your photo reference library.

Fledgling Bluebird with Butterfly

Transfer this line drawing to your prepared surface. Use dark graphite paper, and do a very careful job with all the little lines on the eye, beak, spots and butterfly. Having the tracing paper overlay on the design copy really helps you gauge your accuracy. This · pattern may be hand-traced or photocopied for personal use only. Enlarge at 134 percent to bring it up to full size.

Field Sketches

Thrushes are characterized by lovely spotted breasts.
Some Thrushes lose their spots as they become adults.
They sing spectacularly flute-like notes, memorable and
stirring.

Do you recognize these birds?

THE THRUSH FAMILY

SWAINSON'S THRUSH
Thrushes have large eyes, often
with prominent light
eye-rings.

AMERICAN ROBIN (JUVENILE)
Robins and Bluebirds are more tolerant of humans
than other thrushes that
may be as common,
but are shy and
seldom seen.

HERMIT THRUSH
The shy Hermit
Thrushes winter
here. I see
one come early
for a drink
before things get
busy around the
feeders.

YOUNG EASTERN BLUEBIRD
(HE'S A THRUSH TOO!)
Specially designed nest boxes have
helped this species stage a comeback.

WOOD THRUSH
Wood Thrushes' spots are
large and dark against
the pale breast.

Create Loose, Fluffy Feathers

Base the prepared panel with a mixture of equal parts of April Showers and Wicker. Let dry, sand, and rebase with the same mix. While still wet, drizzle one inch (2.5cm) of Soft Blue in the center of the panel and roll it to blend softly. Then at the bottom of the panel, drizzle on two inches (5.1cm) of Green Olive and one inch (2.5cm) of Sage in two different places. Roll the darker values mostly around the edges of the panel, especially at the bottom. Let dry, spray with Krylon Matte Finish and transfer the drawing to the surface.

1 Base the lighter blue areas with a mixture of Indigo + Cerulean Blue. Add a bit of black to that mix and fill in the darker areas with a no. 4 bright.

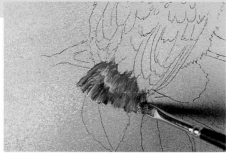

2 Dry the brush and pick up a little dirty white from a dry loading zone. Pull a few short feather lines to separate the tail feathers. Let the lighter feathers be a second, rough row, and add a few lines there too.

Use Tracing Tissue for the Spot Pattern

6 Base the shoulder and scapular area above the left wing with Indigo + Cerulean Blue. Add Raw Umber to the blue mix and continue basing over the right wing. Chop the color on, following the growth direction of the area. Highlight the bottom edges of the area with dirty white. You can touch on the spotting freehand using the corner of the no. 4 bright loaded in a mixture of Raw Sienna + Titanium White. Or you can replace the pattern by tracing it into the wet paint.

7 To replace a complex spot pattern that you want to make really accurate, try this trick. Carefully trace the pattern onto tracing paper (or use the overlay you created when transferring the original design). Cut out the section of pattern you need and center it over the wet paint. With a ballpoint pen, trace over the spots, pressing firmly.

8 Now you can see the spots transferred into the wet paint. It's a cinch now to touch them back in with dirty white. Gently blend into the base coat any that get too light or seem too busy.

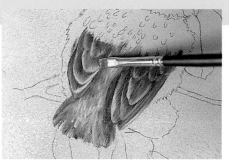

3 Fill in the center of the back with the Indigo + Cerulean Blue mix. Chop the colors in with the chisel for texture. Then fill in the wings sparsely with Raw Umber + Ivory Black. Fill some of the holes with the same blue mix and blend it into the dark. Draw in feather lines with the stylus as you cover them so you don't lose the wing pattern.

4 With a mixture of Raw Sienna + Titanium White, use the chisel to lay in the feather lines. Make them wider on the secondaries, and then blend some of the light value into the feather, using the chisel of the no. 4 bright. I "borrow" about half the width of this margin, and pull the brush with the growth direction in a series of very close, very fine lines. If you can see between these directional lines you need more of them! This step can be handled loosely, even a bit raggedly, since baby birds' feathers are not as groomed and as neat as adults'.

5 Base the fuzzy breast feathers that stick out to the sides with Raw Umber + Titanium White. Fluff the color in, changing the direction of the chisel so that the feathers go in all directions. Wipe the base coat off the brush and pick up white. Go back and highlight with a few more fluffs. Let the brush tracks show.

9 Base the eye-ring with Raw Umber + Titanium White. Fill in the eye with black and highlight with a dot of white. Base the cheek with Raw Umber + Titanium White to a medium warm gray. Base the throat with white. Base the crown with Indigo + Cerulean Blue, with touches of black intermingled. Base the upper mandible and the tip of the lower mandible with Raw Umber. Fill in the gape with a yellowish mix of Cadmium Scarlet + Cadmium Yellow Pale + Raw Sienna to cut the intensity of the stronger colors.

10 Now begin to refine the head area. Cut down a bit on the size of the eye-ring by blending adjacent colors into it. Highlight at the back of the eye-ring with a touch of white on the tip of the round brush. Highlight the cheek with some short choppy strokes of white. Do the same on the crown areas, adding a few smaller spots like those on the back. Finally highlight the edge of the gape with a bit of Cadmium Lemon + Titanium White. Make sure throat feathers fluff softly over the upper edge of the breast. Nape feathering needs to soften gently into the back feathers below it. That's why we paint a bird from tail to head—with each step we can connect and overlay the previous color area.

Paint the Butterfly and Rose

11 Begin basing the Blue Flasher butterfly by placing a mixture of Indigo + Cerulean Blue in the blue areas on the wing and on the thorax. Base the abdomen with black. Base the rest of the wings with a mixture of Raw Sienna + Burnt Sienna. Fill in the small irregular spots with white. A no. 2 bright usually works wonderfully for basing such small, tight areas.

12 Add a little black shading under the edge of the forewing to separate it from the hind wing. Add some additional black shading at the wing edges. Add white highlighting in the middle of the blue areas, laying it on with the brush chisel. Use the round brush to add a few curving lines of very dirty white on the abdomen.

13 Blend the black shading with the growth direction, using light strokes of the small chisel. Now blend the white highlights with the same brush, using it very dry. As you blend, you'll pick up a little light value on the brush. Use this "borrowed" paint to define the margins of the Burnt Sienna wing areas. Pull just a few light lines for direction and to add another value. Blend the highlights on the thorax with stippling of the round brush or by pulling short strokes to make it look fuzzy. Wait to paint the antennae until you've finished the rose.

Final Touches

17 Add these final touches to the rose: bits of Raw Umber here and there to strengthen the Prima Gray; strongest highlights on the petals with white; and if you wish, a bit of additional highlight on the stems or leaflets. But don't get too contrasty or too gaudy. In this painting the rose is not the star. Add white dots inside the butterfly's antennae tips.

18 The dark value on the larger leaves is Ivory Black + Sap Green, and the light is the same Cerulean Blue + Titanium White mix you used for the smaller leaflets. Base the color in very dryly. Begin to blend, pulling from the edge of the leaf to the center, following the growth direction and using the chisel edge. Keep the brush dry, wiping it on a paper towel every few strokes.

19 The small leaf behind the bird's beak should be quite light so the beak contrasts with it. Adjust those values by adding more light if needed. Other leaves can also be highlighted with Cerulean Blue plus more white and reblended with the chisel. Add a central vein line with the same mix, as well as a few side veins. And check where the bird overlaps the leaves: Add a bit more bird fluff if needed to put it back on top.

14 Base the rose petals with a mixture of Cadmium Yellow Pale + Titanium White. Add shadow areas with Prima Gray. Cover the graphite lines between petals to help blend them into the paint, and then draw the petal line back with the stylus for a guide while shading and highlighting. Base stems and leaflets with a dark mix of Ivory Black + Sap Green in the dark shadow areas. Use a light mix of Cerulean Blue + Titanium White for light values.

15 Blend between the values on the leaves and stem. Add additional highlights with a lighter value of Cerulean Blue + Titanium White. Blend the shading into the rose petals, following the growth direction. Lay on initial accent color with Burnt Sienna. Establish highlight areas with a little clean white.

16 Blend Burnt Sienna areas with the growth. Begin to strengthen some of them with Winsor Red + Titanium White plus a bit of Raw Sienna to control intensity. Add this mix in very tiny areas and in sparse amounts. Blend highlighting on leaves and stems. Choose the strongest areas of light on the petals and rehighlight them with more clean white. The large, central petal should dominate. When you are ready, you can add the antennae lines with black.

Try a Different Butterfly

Wouldn't this Southern Dogface be great on the Goldfinch piece?
Or how about it instead of the wren on the sprinkling can?

1. Base the yellow area with Cadmium Yellow Pale. Place shading on top with Raw Sienna.

2. Blend shading. Highlight yellows with Cadmium Lemon + Titanium White. Base darks with Burnt Umber + Raw Umber.

3. Blend highlights. Add fine Raw Sienna section lines (with no. 4 bright, not round). Add spots (little doughnuts) with round brush. Tap on yellow margins with Cadmium Yellow Pale using round brush.

Sherry C. Nelson

⑨ Northern Cardinals and Spring Blossoms

Materials

To paint the background, you'll need:
- Hardboard (Masonite) panel, 12" x 16" (30.5cm x 40.6cm), ⅛" (.3cm) thick
- Sponge roller
- Acrylic paints (by Accent)
  Wild Honey
  New Leaf
- Paper towels
- Protected work surface
- 220-grit wet/dry sandpaper
- Krylon Matte Finish, #1311
- Disposable palette for oils
- Palette knife
- Odorless thinner
- Cobalt siccative (optional)
- Oil Paints
  Raw Umber
  Sap Green
- Cheesecloth

To paint the Cardinals and spring blossoms, you'll need:
- Oil paints
  Ivory Black
  Titanium White
  Raw Umber
  Burnt Umber
  Raw Sienna
  Burnt Sienna
  Yellow Ochre
  Cadmium Yellow Pale
  Winsor Red
  Cadmium Scarlet
  Alizarin Crimson
  Cadmium Lemon
  Sap Green
- Brushes
  nos. 2, 4 and 6 red sable brights
  no. 0 or 1 red sable round
- Odorless thinner
- Cobalt siccative (optional)
- Palette knife
- Paper towels
- Disposable palette for oils
- White graphite paper
- Tracing paper
- Ballpoint pen
- Stylus

The Cardinal was voted state bird of seven states—more than any other species—and this stunning redbird certainly deserves the recognition. It is a skilled vocalist as well, with more than two dozen variations on its rich whistled song. The heavy conical bill gives away its membership in the finch family and makes it a regular consumer of sunflower seeds at winter feeders. Just because we think of Cardinals and Christmas holly as an automatic twosome doesn't mean we can't paint these birds in a spray of showy spring blossoms.

This sycamore snag makes a great place for peanut butter. I use an old spatula to coat the bark. A nearby twig holds an orange slice. Both will tempt birds of many kinds, including this male Northern Cardinal.

PHOTOS BY DEBORAH A. GALLOWAY

And here is his sweetie, waiting for her turn. She's just as beautiful in her own understated way. After all, she can't be too gaudy; she needs to blend with her surroundings while caring for her brood.

Northern Cardinals and Spring Blossoms

Transfer this drawing to the prepared background with white graphite paper. Watch
those shapes, especially for the eyes, beaks
and feather lines! This pattern may be hand-
traced or photocopied for personal use only.
Enlarge at 200 percent to bring it to full size.

Field Sketches

The Finch family is the largest bird family, with over eighty species. Often called redbirds, Cardinals have conspicuous crests and the flashes of red that are their distinctive trademarks.

PYRRHULOXIA (PIER-UH-LOX'-EE-UH)
...exas, New Mexico and Arizona, ...ders with the Northern Cardinal.

The bill is strongly curved like a Parrot's, and it's more yellow too.

RED-CRESTED CARDINAL
Native to south America, can also be seen in Hawaii, where this imported species is thriving.

Upper mandible much straighter

FEMALE NORTHERN CARDINAL (CARDINALIS CARDINALIS)
Cardinals are closely related to Grosbeaks and Buntings, seedeaters with heavy bills.

Recognize this bird? It's a teenage Northern Cardinal, still in his adolescent plumage, complete with black beak!

Start with the Female Cardinal

This background is prepared just like the Goldfinch background. See pages 12 and 13 for step-by-step instructions for preparing it. When you finish the background, carefully transfer the drawing, paying particular attention to the details.

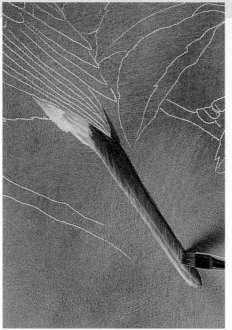

1 Ladies first. Base the top side of the tail with Burnt Sienna + Winsor Red. Base the underside with Raw Umber + Titanium White. With the gray mix on a no. 6 bright, pull the long feather line from tip to base. Shade the under tail coverts with Burnt Umber next to the wing tip. Soften and fluff the shading. Highlight the tips of the under tail feathers with a little clean white.

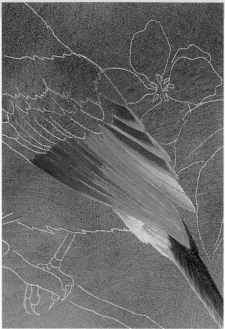

2 Base the primaries and secondaries as shown here, using Burnt Sienna + Winsor Red for the red areas and Raw Umber + Titanium White for the gray areas. Draw with the stylus any feather lines that get lost.

Paint the Breast and Head

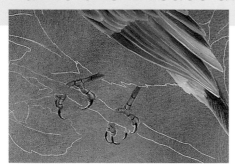

6 Base the feet with sparse Burnt Sienna. Add narrow lines of dirty white with the no. 4 bright down the center shaft of the leg and on the toes. Blend the light line by tapping on it with a dry chisel. Add detail lines and toenails with thinned Raw Umber.

7 Base the dark area under the wing with Raw Umber plus a tad of Sap Green. Base the area between the legs and behind the bottom leg with Yellow Ochre + Titanium White. Add a little Cadmium Yellow Pale and a smidgen of Cadmium Scarlet to the mix and base halfway up the breast. Finally, with Raw Sienna + Cadmium Scarlet and a little of the Yellow Ochre + Titanium White, base the remaining part, the reddest area.

8 Now with the no. 6 bright begin to blend where the colors meet, softening one into the next, but not blending so as to lose any of the values. Use the chisel and chop into the surface, following the growth direction and letting the brush tracks show. Shade with a little Raw Umber on the outer edge of the area, and blend that to connect with the other values. Finally, accent the red area with Burnt Sienna + Winsor Red, working the color in with the same kind of texture strokes.

3 Blend with the growth direction between the red and gray areas within each feather. Pick up dirty white on the no. 6 bright and pull the feather lines from tip to base. Shade under the edges of the secondaries and between the secondaries and primaries with Burnt Umber. Then soften it into the base coat.

4 Base the coverts with the same mixes as you used for the primaries and secondaries. Lay the red in the shadow area of each feather and the gray around the margins. Blend lightly between the values when all the feathers have been based. Add a little Burnt Umber shading on a few of the feathers. With just a little dirty white, lighten the edges of a few feathers.

5 Base in the shoulder area above the wing with Raw Umber + Titanium White. Shade at the back of the bird's neck with Raw Umber.

9 Use the round brush and Raw Umber + Titanium White for the eye-ring. Fill in the eye with black and highlight it with a dot of white. Apply the black mask with a small bright, narrowing down the eye-ring as you fill in the area. Use the chisel to keep the edges of the mask notched and uneven. Base the bottom of the beak with Winsor Red + Burnt Sienna. Base the top half with the same mix with a bit of white added to lighten the value.

10 Using the no. 2 bright, shade a little with Raw Umber at the edges of the beak and between the mandibles. With the round brush, tap on a dab or two of white on the bottom of the beak and a few more on the top. Wipe the brush, flatten the tip, and stipple to soften and to get a value gradation. Base the red crest with Winsor Red + Burnt Sienna, the cheek with Yellow Ochre + Titanium White plus a smidgen of Cadmium Scarlet, and the nape with Raw Umber plus a little Sap Green and white.

11 Now begin to connect the color areas, blending where they meet with a small chisel. Soften the surrounding color into the black mask, and narrow the rest of the eye-ring as you work. Highlight with a little Yellow Ochre + Titanium White behind the eye. Add small black flecks around the eye with just a bit of paint on the tip of the round brush. Highlight the nape, using a small bright with a little dirty white.

Paint the Male from Tail to Head

12 The dark value of the male Cardinal's tail is Burnt Umber. The outer light edge of the feathers is Winsor Red + Cadmium Scarlet. Fill in the middle area with Winsor Red + Burnt Sienna. Base the foot with Burnt Sienna and apply the light lines as you did for the female using Yellow Ochre + Titanium White.

13 Using the dry chisel edge, blend the larger feathers using short, close brush strokes. Add very dirty white feather lines and center shaft lines. If you wish, add another detail here. Imitate the look of feather splits by pulling a narrow line of Ivory Black + Raw Umber at the same angle as the natural growth direction. Soften the light on the foot and add the detail lines and toenails with slightly thinned black and the round brush.

14 Begin laying in the breast colors, first with the darkest value, Burnt Umber. Next to that apply Alizarin Crimson, then Winsor Red and finally Yellow Ochre in the central part of the area. Lay the color on with choppy strokes of the no. 6 bright, and follow the natural growth direction.

17 With a dry brush, begin to connect the colors where they meet, blending with the chisel in the growth direction. Remember that the cheek area growth sweeps back rather than down, and adjust your brush movement accordingly.

18 Now highlight a last time with Yellow Ochre + Titanium White on the cheek and the top of the crest. Add a little paint, blend it to soften, and then lighten once more, if needed. Also add bits of final shading with Burnt Umber or Burnt Umber + Ivory Black in the crevices at the nape and under the point of the crest. These small areas of darker darks will add to the contrast and drama of the painting far out of proportion to their size.

15 Use a dry chisel, and flip and fluff the colors as you blend. Shade with Burnt Umber + Ivory Black at the outer edges and behind the branch. Soften the lighter values of red over the shading. Highlight in the breast with a little Yellow Ochre + Titanium White, and fluff that color to overlay the base coat. Pull a few bits of feathery fluff over the top of the leg.

16 Base the male's eye-ring with Raw Umber + Titanium White, and fill in the eye with black. Highlight the eye with a dot of white. Add the black mask, narrowing the eye-ring as you work. Base the beak with a mixture of Cadmium Scarlet + Cadmium Yellow Pale + Titanium White. Keep working on the eye-ring size until it's very narrow. Shade the beak with sparse Raw Umber at the outer edges and between the mandibles. Dab on the white with the point of the round, and stipple it as you did on the female. Blend with the flattened tip to achieve a really nice gradation, and then rehighlight with a bit more white. Base the rest of the head with the same colors you used for the breast: Burnt Umber in the darkest areas, followed by Alizarin Crimson, Winsor Red and Yellow Ochre.

Pay Attention to Details

Transfer the line drawing perfectly, and then follow it exactly. Even a 1/16" (.2cm) or 1/8" (.3cm) change in a single line can make your bird look like a different species.

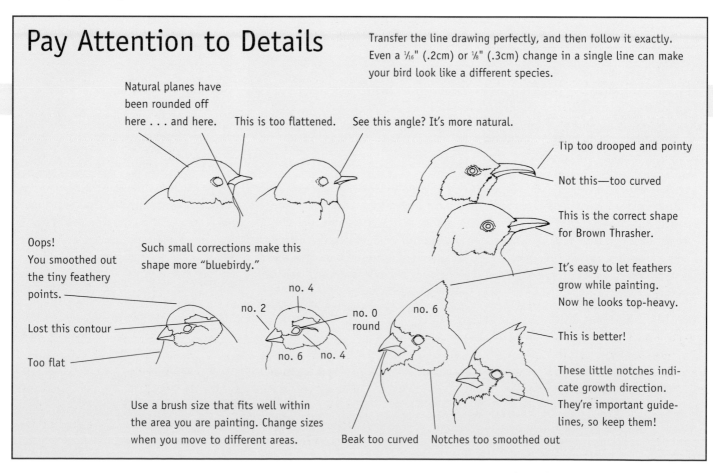

Natural planes have been rounded off here . . . and here.

This is too flattened.

See this angle? It's more natural.

Oops! You smoothed out the tiny feathery points.

Lost this contour

Too flat

Such small corrections make this shape more "bluebirdy."

no. 2
no. 4
no. 6 no. 4
no. 0 round
no. 6

Use a brush size that fits well within the area you are painting. Change sizes when you move to different areas.

Beak too curved   Notches too smoothed out

Tip too drooped and pointy

Not this—too curved

This is the correct shape for Brown Thrasher.

It's easy to let feathers grow while painting. Now he looks top-heavy.

This is better!

These little notches indicate growth direction. They're important guidelines, so keep them!

Create Blossoms Several at a Time

19 The dark value on the blossoms is Ivory Black + Sap Green, applied quite sparsely. The light value is white. The dark value on the leaves is the same as for the blossoms. For the lighter leaf areas, use Sap Green + Cadmium Lemon + Raw Sienna from the Foliage Mix. There are several steps involved with the blossoms, building toward the lightest values, so be sure to begin with a sparse base coat. Too much paint at this stage leads to muddy messes later. Lay on the dark underside of the branch with Raw Umber and the light value with white.

20 Blend the branch colors with the chisel edge of a bright held parallel to the branch. Bounce the brush between the two colors, leaving little brush tracks. This easy method will give a realistic look.

21 Blend the values on the blossom petals where the colors meet with the flat side of a no. 4 bright. Pull the paint in short strokes, and crisscross the strokes as you make them so the texture does not go all one way. I usually paint several blossoms at a time to speed up the process.

Build Final Highlights

24 Now add the tiny center dots. Four or five Cadmium Yellow Pale dots go in close around the center. Farther out on the petals add some dots with Burnt Sienna. You can thin the paint if you wish; I usually apply it unthinned so the dots stand up from the surface a little.

25 Blend the leaves with the chisel edge of a no. 6 bright. Pull from the edge toward the center, making the strokes very close together and following the direction of the side-vein structure of the leaf. Are you lifting paint and making stripes in the leaf? Lower the angle of the brush to the surface. When you hold the chisel straight up, it tends to dig up the paint as it slides along.

26 Add the center vein structure with the light value mix. Always pull the big center vein from the stem end of the leaf, where it is fatter, and let it narrow as you slide the brush down the leaf.

22 Now rehighlight with clean white. Lay the color on firmly with a dry brush. When you apply paint firmly, it looks like there's a lot of it, but really it's just sitting on the surface and keeping a good clean look.

23 Thin a little of the light value leaf mix. Use a round brush to make tiny green lines radiating from the blossom centers. If they don't show up, perhaps the value is too dark. Add a little Sap Green and more white to the mix to brighten it.

27 Building final highlights in a painting is often easier when the piece is totally dry. Since cobalt siccative, which I use every time I paint, will dry a painting overnight, it's no problem to wait a bit. You can see how much brighter these blossoms are becoming, since I am putting the strongest white highlights on a dry surface. Apply a small amount of paint, wipe the brush very dry, and then blend the paint exactly as if the surface were wet. It really adds spark to the painting.

28 As reds dry, they tend to become dull. I like to wait overnight and then go back with the same reds I used before to build in some real knockout spark without making it too intense. Here I'm adding Winsor Red in small amounts and then blending it with a dry brush into the dry surface of the bird. No need to be nervous about this. If you don't like it, you can simply wipe it off the dry surface with a bit of thinner on a paper towel. It's a fun, no-risk way to add extra oomph to your work.

Sherry C Nelson

⑩ Bewick's Wren and Johnny-Jump-Ups

In a garden setting, amidst the flower beds and hanging baskets and digging tools, you notice the wren last of all. Bouncing around, busy looking and eating and exploring, you'd think they'd stand out. But their earth tones meld right in. You have to look twice to find a Wren. The one I chose to paint is pronounced like the car: Buick, not Bee-wick. You can enjoy their company more common-ly in the Southwest than the eastern states, where their numbers are declining.

Materials

To paint the background, you'll need:
- Hardboard (Masonite) panel, 11" x 14" (27.9cm x 35.6cm), ⅛" (.3cm) thick
- Sponge roller
- Acrylic paints (all by Accent)
  Light Mushroom
  True Purple
  Off White
- Paper towels
- Protected work surface
- 220-grit wet/dry sandpaper
- Krylon Matte Finish, #1311
- Disposable palette for oils
- Palette knife
- Cobalt siccative (optional)
- Odorless thinner
- Oil paints
  Raw Umber
  Sap Green
- Cheesecloth

To paint the Wren and Johnny-jump-ups, you'll need:
- Oil Paints
  Ivory Black
  Titanium White
  Raw Umber
  Raw Sienna
  Burnt Umber
  Cadmium Lemon
  Sap Green
  Purple Madder Alizarin
  Cadmium Yellow
- Brushes
  nos. 2, 4, 6 and 8 red sable brights
  no. 0 red sable round
- Odorless thinner
- Cobalt siccative (optional)
- Palette knife
- Paper towels
- Disposable palette for oils
- Dark graphite paper
- Tracing paper
- Ballpoint pen
- Stylus

Here's the Bewick's, who came to the window during a snowstorm for a handout. Wrens are not seedeaters, but you can entice them with suet blocks and mealworms in a cup feeder. During extreme cold this little bird would eat constantly throughout the day.

Lucky me, with a beautiful Carolina Wren in hand. I had just extricated this guy from a mist net at a banding station. The bird will be weighed, measured and have a numbered band placed on one leg. Banding records have helped de-termine the lifestyle and migration patterns of many species that were little known.

PHOTOS BY DEBORAH A. GALLOWAY

Bewick's Wren and Johnny-Jump-Ups

Transfer this line drawing to the prepared
surface with dark graphite paper. Take your
time, especially on the Wren, to get a really
accurate transfer. This pattern may be hand-
traced or photocopied for personal use only.
Enlarge at 143 percent to bring it to full size.

Field Sketches

There are nine Wrens in North America: these five; the Bewick's we're painting; the Carolina I'm holding in the reference photo; and two more, the Marsh Wren and the Sedge Wren.

All Wrens share an active, inquisitive lifestyle and abound with aggressive energy. They are quick to protect their territory and noisy about it too.

ROCK WREN
Often does "knee bends" when disturbed and bobs its head. Found on arid slopes and in dry washes in the West.

HOUSE WREN
A summer resident in most of the United States. It's common, with an exuberant song!

CACTUS WREN
Our largest wren at 8½" (21.6cm). Nests are often a bulky mass of grasses and twigs in the top of a cholla. The cactus spines help deter would-be predators.

CANYON WREN
While we were building, our resident Canyon Wren came in to check out the construction. It sings the most beautiful song of all, echoing off cliffs and down the canyon. Hear this song and you're hooked. The Canyon Wren turned this hiker into a birder.

White throat and rust breast are distinctive.

Tail's often cocked up, especially during singing!

Our littlest Wren at 4" (10.2cm).

WINTER WREN
Look for this guy in the southeast United States in winter; the Northeast and West Coast in the summer. He wins the "shortest tail" award.

Emphasize Details on the Wren

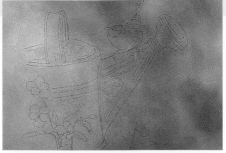

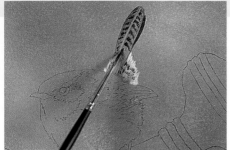

This background is prepared as a wet-on-wet with oil antiquing. Base then rebase with Light Mushroom. While wet, drizzle a 2" (5.1cm) stripe of True Purple in the center of the surface and roll it around to soften and blend. Then, in an area where there's no purple, drizzle about an inch (2.5cm) of Off White. Roll the roller on a pad of paper towel to remove the excess paint, then roll it into the white and move it around a bit on the surface, just here and there, like you would do for highlighting. When the surface is dry, antique with Raw Umber and a mixture of Raw Umber and Sap Green. Let dry and spray with Krylon Matte Finish.

1 Base the Wren's tail and under tail coverts with a dark gray mixture of Ivory Black + Raw Umber plus a tad of white in the dark areas. Use the same mix, with more white added, in the light areas. Blend the light tips of the under tail feathers into the dark base with a small chisel. Base the partial feather showing under the edge of the tail with Ivory Black + Raw Umber. Lay a dirty white central shaft line in the center of the main tail feather.

2 Since the tiny markings can be tricky, you may feel more confident about their placement if you etch the pattern into the wet paint with the stylus before you start painting them. If you don't like the pattern when you finish, just brush back over the large feather and try again. When you are happy with the pattern you've drawn, thin a little Ivory Black + Raw Umber and lay in the tiny markings with the point of the no. 0 round. Make them with groupings of individual lines joined together. Review the Downy Woodpecker project, pages 38-45, if you've forgotten how.

Refine the Features

6 Base the eye-ring with Raw Umber + Titanium White. Fill in the eye with black, and highlight it with a tiny dot of white. Add the black eyeline in front of and behind the eye with the round brush. With a clean no. 2 bright, lay the jagged eyebrow of white above the eye and the beak. Base the lower mandible with Ivory Black + Raw Umber and the upper with the same mix with a bit of white added. Using the round brush and slightly thinned black, apply the rest of the detail, both above the white eyebrow and below the beak in the little markings that are referred to as "whisker marks."

7 Fill in the throat area with clean white. Base the cheek of the bird with a medium value gray made with Ivory Black + Raw Umber + Titanium White. Narrow the eye-ring at the back, so the widest part is a half-moon under the eye. Connect the throat and breast areas by blending where they meet. Highlight the beak with white. Base the back, crown and neck of the wren with Burnt Umber + Raw Umber. Soften where this new color meets the gray on the cheek and neck. Blend a bit into the white above the beak and add a bit of black detail with the round brush to define the cheek area.

8 Highlight with dirty white on the crown of the bird with short strokes of the no. 2 bright. Pull a little of the Burnt Umber mix up onto the base of the tail, fluffing it with short strokes. Add a drop of odorless thinner to a little Ivory Black + Raw Umber. Using the round brush, add the tiny dark markings at the base of the tail and on the wing feathers. Add any other markings you need to define the cheek. Finally, using the round brush loaded with a bit of dirty white, touch the tiny spotting along the edges of the primary wing feathers. It's like doing a dotted line on top of the line you did with the chisel edge.

3 Base the primary wing feathers with Ivory Black + Raw Umber on the bottom of the stack and the same mix plus a little white added for a lighter gray at the top of the stack. Blend where the values meet. Draw in feather lines with a stylus. Now, using dirty white on a small bright, lightly pull the feather lines from tip to base on top of the stylus lines. Base the little covert rows with Burnt Umber + Raw Sienna. Draw in the feather lines with the stylus.

4 Using dirty white on a no. 2 bright, touch on the tiny covert lines to cover your stylus marks. Curve them a bit, working with the bird rotated. Base the breast using Ivory Black + Raw Umber + Titanium White for the darker shadow areas and Raw Sienna + Titanium White for the lighter central areas. Chop on the colors with the growth direction of the feathers, and let some brush marks show for texture.

5 Add white highlighting in the central area of the breast. Blend with the choppy chisel, following the growth direction. Add more and fluff it out until you are satisfied with the lightness and gradations. Now fluff over the edge of the wing, using either a no. 2 bright or the round brush.

Perfecting Detail Markings

How do yours look? They may seem insignificant, but the markings can make the bird!

1. Like this?

Oops! Markings cross the central feather shaft. A no-no.

A bit heavy handed and too big

They are all straight, and all lines are the same length.

These cover the feather lines and are too rigidly lined up in rows like a marching band.

2. Still not quite right

Too random. Natural patterning is lost.

Wrong shape! A Wren is not a Thrush.

Too much space between rows

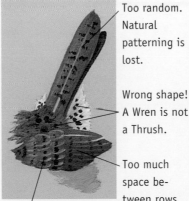

Stacked on top of one another!

3. Yes!

Tiny feathers = tiny markings!

Study the natural variation of placement, shape and size and emulate that.

Central shaft separates markings correctly.

Random, softer, but still a good pattern.

Note how markings are offset like bricks, not stacked directly on top of each other.

A bug gives your bird a focus. They're fun to paint, too!

Base body parts with black.

Highlight body with Sap Green + Cadmium Lemon. Fill in wings with Raw Sienna.

Stipple highlight on body. Outline wings with Purple Madder Alizarin. Add white lines on the body, and use black to paint teeny angular legs.

Start the Watering Can

9 Using the no. 8 bright and very dry paint, scruff in the dark and light areas on the spout of the old sprinkling can. Use Ivory Black + Raw Umber + Burnt Umber for some of the darks and just Ivory Black + Raw Umber for others. Add white to the Ivory Black + Raw Umber mix for a medium gray for the light areas. Keep the paint dry. Do not cover the surfaces entirely.

10 Now you can begin to refine a bit, using stronger darks and lights. As you add paint, you'll gradually fill those sparse areas. Use the same darks as before. When you lay them on again, it will have the effect of making that area darker. Add more white to the light mix for a lighter value.

11 Add the final highlights using Cadmium Lemon with clean white, and in the smallest areas, just sparks of pure white. Use the brush a bit roughly and don't worry about blending too smoothly. This old can was dull and pitted. Visible brush strokes enhance the antique look. When the last lights are on, use the round brush and a dark mix to add the holes in the spout.

Create the Metal Texture

14 Now you can begin to strengthen the darks by adding a bit more paint with pressure. Remember, you can always put more paint on. It's much easier than trying to fix a muddy mess caused by using too much paint from the start. When stronger darks have been added, put a bit more white in the light value gray you used for the based areas and begin to build smaller but lighter lights. Raw Sienna accents are nice to relieve the gray tones and warm them up. Accents are best when added in the middle value areas.

15 Begin adding those final lights. Use Cadmium Lemon with the clean white at first. Then spark it with pure white in tiny areas. If you wish you can frame the piece so only a portion of the can shows, as is painted here, or you can complete the left side of the can and add a partial handle, as I did in the original. Since the bird is the active, moving part of the painting, it easily carries the focus, allowing the other elements to be cropped as you choose.

16 Base the stems and leaves with two values of green. For the dark, use Ivory Black + Sap Green; for the light, a dark value from the Foliage Mix. Base the purple petals of the heartsease (called Johnny-jump-ups because they grow so quickly) with Purple Madder Alizarin, leaving a narrow outline to be filled in with white. Base the middle two petals with Cadmium Lemon and the larger bottom petal with Cadmium Yellow.

12 Base the wren's feet with Ivory Black + Raw Umber. Lay a fine dirty white line down the center of the toes and the shaft of the leg with a no. 2 bright. Blend by tapping the dry brush on the line, pushing it into the base coat a bit. Add detail with slightly thinned black and the round brush. Fluff the breast feathers over the top of each leg. And check the bird's breast. If it touches the spout, add a bit of feathering to place the bird in front of the spout.

13 Now you can begin to work on the rest of the old can. Rough in the darks and lights with the same mixes and methods you used for the spout. Work loosely and sparsely. If you want to paint over the flowers you can retransfer them later, when the can is dry. If not, go around them as I did here.

17 Blend the green values with the growth direction of the leaves and stems. Add a central light-value vein in each small leaf, using the chisel edge. Begin detailing the purple petals by blending the narrow white band toward the center of the flower using the chisel of the no. 2 bright. Make very tight strokes, as if blending a leaf. Highlight the tips of the middle petals with a bit of white. Using the round brush, thin a bit of Purple Madder Alizarin and add the fine lines pulling from the center of the yellow petals outward. With the same color, stipple a bit of purple at the bottom of each of the darker yellow petals. Finally, add two tiny strokes of white and a dab or two of Cadmium Yellow at the centers.

18 Load just a little Ivory Black + Raw Umber onto a no. 6 bright and lay on shadows under and around the can. Soften them out with a bit of cheesecloth, blending lightly to get a value gradation from the can to the end of the shadow. Add a few grasses with various values of greens at the bases of the flower stems and around the bottom of the sprinkling can.

19 Last, add the little insect. It's fun to give the wren something to look for. Keep it subtle! If both the viewer and the bird have to hunt a little, it'll be that much more realistic.

Sherry C. Nelson

⑪ Barn Swallow

My mom is a birder and my dad is birder tolerant. Barn Swallows like to nest under the eaves of my parents' condo, creating a little messy disorder. This was not a problem until they chose the porch light directly above the door. Dad would not negotiate and neither would the Swallows. No sooner would he remove the mud foundation than they'd have another started. He wrapped the lamp in plastic; they built on top. Finally, Dad bought an identical porch light and mounted it over the flower bed. It was accepted, so Mom and I can enjoy those funny babies peering over the edge of their nest atop the decoy lamp.

Materials

To paint the background, you'll need
- Hardboard (Masonite) panel, 12" x 16" (30.5cm x 40.6cm) or 14" x 18" (35.6cm x 45.7cm), ⅛" (.3cm) thick
- Sponge roller
- Acrylic paints (by Accent)
  Wicker
  Light Stoneware Blue
- Paper towels
- Protected work surface
- 220-grit wet/dry sandpaper
- Krylon Matte Finish, #1311

To paint the Barn Swallow, you'll need
- Oil paints
  Ivory Black
  Titanium White
  Raw Umber
  Raw Sienna
  Burnt Sienna
  Burnt Umber
  Cerulean Blue
  Indigo
  Prussian Blue
  Cadmium Yellow Pale
- Brushes
  nos. 2, 4, 6 and 8 red sable brights
  no. 0 or 1 red sable round
- Odorless thinner
- Cobalt siccative (optional)
- Palette knife
- Paper towels
- Disposable palette for oils
- Dark and white graphite paper
- Tracing paper
- Ballpoint pen
- Stylus
- 1" (2.5cm) synthetic-bristle mop brush or any old clean brush that's fluffy and soft
- Cheesecloth

A Tree Swallow in hand: a wonderful chance to observe the action of light on the dark blue feathers. The iridescence is a dynamic, changing quality, a challenge to paint—not to mention the long wings and intricate feathering.

Here's a group of migrating Swallows to study. The brown ones are "birds of the year," those young ones who have not molted into their first full adult plumage. Even so, a few show patches of blue. By next Spring, when they return, they'll be decked out in all their finery. The species: Tree Swallows. Barn Swallows would have longer forked tails and rust accents to the plumage.

Barn Swallow

Transfer this line drawing to the prepared
surface using dark graphite. Omit the transfer of the cobweb and the broken window
pieces until the dark shadowing is complete
and dry. Then transfer those details onto the
dark with white graphite. This pattern may
be hand-traced or photocopied for personal
use only. Enlarge at 200 percent to bring it
up to full size.

Field Sketches

All our native cavity-nesting birds must compete with Starlings and House Sparrows for homes. Add a few bird-houses to your outdoor decor!

    Tree Swallows form flocks numbering in the thousands during migration.

SWALLOWS

BARN SWALLOWS
Build mud nests under the eaves and line them with feathers and horsehair.

TREE SWALLOW
Cavity nesters, these birds will use a nest box right in the yard.

swallow wing shape is adapted to swift, fluid flight, with amazing maneuverability.

slender bodies, and long and pointed wings.

VIOLET-GREEN SWALLOW
The adept, darting flight enables them to catch insects by the hundreds on the wing.

Use Blues on the Tail, Wings and Back

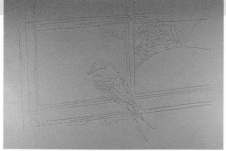

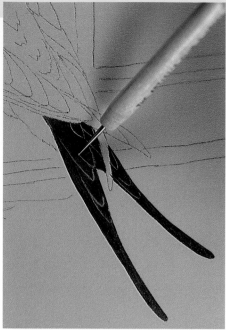

Base a prepared panel with one coat of Wicker, using the sponge roller. Let dry, sand lightly and dust off. Recoat the surface with Wicker. If you wish, you can roll a 3" (7.6cm) stripe of Light Stoneware Blue across the top third of the surface. Blend the Light Stoneware Blue into the Wicker by rolling along the line where the colors meet. They will just fade together. Let dry, then spray with Krylon Matte Finish.

1 Base the swallow's tail with a mixture of Indigo + Cerulean Blue. Draw in stylus lines as you cover the graphite feather lines.

2 Wipe the brush dry and load a sparse amount of Raw Sienna + Titanium White—mostly Raw Sienna—on the brush. Pull the feather lines, covering the stylus lines. Then base the wings with Ivory Black + Raw Umber, and again, use the stylus to draw in the lines as you cover them. Be careful—the lay of the long wing feathers is easily distorted.

Paint the Breast and Head

6 Wash the blues out of the brights with odorless thinner, and dry them well on paper towels. Using the no. 6 bright, lay on Titanium White + Raw Sienna on the under tail coverts and Raw Sienna + Cadmium Yellow Pale on the breast area. Use the chisel and work with the growth direction. At the edges of the breast, add a bit of shading with Burnt Sienna. Chop it into the surface to blend. Base the single visible toe with Ivory Black + Raw Umber, and highlight with a bit of white.

7 Base the eye-ring with Raw Umber + Titanium White, using the round brush. Wash the round in thinner, dry it off, then fill in the eye with clean black. Highlight with a dot of white. Now base the black patch around the eye and between the eye and beak with Ivory Black plus a bit of Raw Umber to speed drying time. Base the rusty areas on the face with Burnt Sienna and the crown patch with Raw Sienna. Add the small dashes of white below the chin patch.

8 Fill in the remaining head area with Indigo + Cerulean Blue, chopping lightly in the growth direction to connect to the other color areas. Add a bit of white highlight on the beak.

3 Lay in all the narrow margins on the primaries and secondaries with a no. 4 bright, using dry Raw Sienna plus a bit of white. Add center shaft lines on some of the larger feathers. Notice how dark the feather lines are. If you outline all these with a whiter mix, it will make the bird look like a zebra. When the feather lines are complete, add some directional lines on the inner half of some of the larger feathers, using Cerulean Blue + Titanium White plus a tad of Prussian Blue on a good no. 4 bright. Just put the bright blue in a few close lines in the fattest part, so it looks as though the light is catching the rounded, upper part of each feather.

4 Base the wing coverts with Indigo + Cerulean Blue at the bottom, gradually changing the color to a larger proportion of Cerulean Blue on the top row. Draw in stylus lines, then replace them with Raw Sienna plus a tad of white, using the small bright and pulling from the tip toward the base of the feather.

5 Base the back with Indigo plus a tad of Cerulean Blue. Shade next to the wing with a little black. Chop the colors a bit with the chisel to get some fluffy texture started. Highlight with Cerulean Blue + Titanium White + Prussian Blue, chopping in short brush tracks for texture and iridescence. Work a few feather strokes at a time, so you don't lose control and get too many strokes and too much paint. It will only take a little for the effect you want.

9 Now highlight with Cerulean Blue + Prussian Blue plus a bit of white on the blue areas of the head. Chop lightly, and don't use much paint. A little of this strong blue mix will go a long way. Use a little bit to accent the roundness of the neck feathers where they are fluffed up. Work a few blue strokes into the edges of the Raw Sienna crown patch to meld that color softly into the blues. Don't blend a lot here, or you'll get a muddy green.

10 Wash the window frame with dirty white, slightly thinned, on your largest bright. As you work the thin paint up to the graphite lines, you can incorporate some of that color into the paint mix to gray it. Don't worry about removing it all at this point. When everything has been whitewashed, streak and tap on some rough, old looking stains and wood grain with Raw Umber and Raw Umber + Ivory Black.

11 Begin to accent some of the white areas with stains of Raw Sienna. Approach this more loosely. Try softening some strong areas with cheesecloth, tapping the brush for texture, dabbing with the brush corner for old nail holes—anything to get that aged, peeling-paint look.

Texture the Old Window Frame

12 Now begin to develop the left edges of the frame. Highlight the two narrow strips where the light is hitting strongly. Add strong Raw Umber under the window ledge, roughing it on with the large bright. Then soften it out into the background with paper towels or a pad of cheesecloth, lightening it in the middle to the lower left of the bird. Add the left outside part of the frame with thinned Raw Umber and highlight it with a little thinned Raw Umber + Titanium White.

13 When the window frame is complete, fill in the window areas with Burnt Umber + Ivory Black and Raw Umber + Ivory Black. Alternating between the two mixes, apply the paint dryly and firmly. Remember: Apply small amounts of paint with pressure, and you'll get better coverage. As you work up to the frame areas, cut into the frame here and there to roughen and "chip" it. If the idea of doing all this around the wet frame and wet bird worries you, simply wait overnight for the paint to dry and then do it.

14 Now that all is filled in, use a soft pad of cheesecloth to soften the brush strokes. You want a deep, rich, velvety soft look to this shadow area. Pat, don't wipe, to prevent visible strokes and lines in the color.

Add the Glass

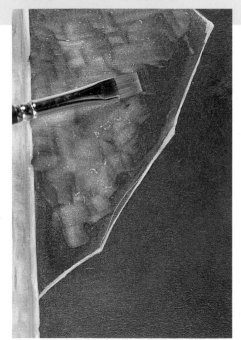

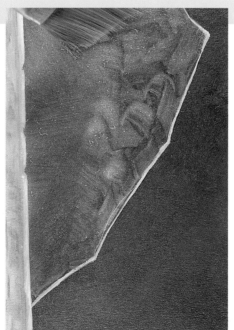

17 This is the most exciting part and the easiest! Simply make a superthin mix of Raw Sienna plus a little white using odorless thinner. Use a no. 8 bright and apply just a wash of it on the "glass."

18 Now, quick—before the thinner sets up—grab a fluffy old brush and whisk it over the brush marks to smooth them out, leaving just a haze of color. You can apply the edge of the glass with the round brush and Raw Sienna + Titanium White either before or after you do the glass. Waiting until after allows you to clean up a little if your mopping gets out of hand.

15 When working around the bird, set a clean side of the pad down and push gently away from the bird—not enough to disturb the paint, but to keep it from getting up onto the blue feathering. With cobalt siccative in the earth colors, it will dry quickly. Wait overnight for the paint to dry completely before proceeding.

16 With white graphite paper, transfer the window lines and the cobweb. Make a very thin mix of Burnt Umber plus a little white. Use this mix on the round brush to lay the cobweb lines on top of the graphite lines. Don't add too much white to the mix; the lines should be rather dull, as would befit an old dusty web. Vary the values of the mix too. Some parts of the web could well be dark and more shadowy looking than others.

Photography as a Reference

If you like painting realistically, you'll need good photos to jog your creativity. Shots of flowers, blossoming trees and even neat old stuff like the sprinkling can, garden gate and old window sill will be a tremendous resource for you.

Begin now to accumulate a reference file of photos of everything you may ever want to paint. A camera is as much a part of my painting world as a sketchbook, and it's quicker too. From bugs to birds, from blossoms to barns, photographs help me remember all those neat things I'll paint when I have a little time.

Even the simple point-and-shoot cameras can be a godsend. Get one with a macro capacity. That means you can come in tight and close for all the complex detail in a flower center or a branch of leaves on which to perch your next bird.

Most of the wonderful bird photos you see in the wildlife magazines are taken by skilled photographers with expensive gear that's beyond the budget of the average artist. But don't give up. Even a distant shot of a bird that won't qualify for publi-

cation can be a great help as a painting reference. And you can improve the quality of your bird reference shots by working from a blind, at banding stations where birds can be seen in hand, at zoos and at aviaries where you can get close to your subject.

Because birds are flighty and fast and don't take time to pose, only rarely do you get a photo so good that you could paint from it directly. You need to back up your photography with good observation skills and field sketches. I study and observe birds every day. I use good 10 x 40 close-focus birding binoculars to put me in their world without intruding. The more I watch, the more I understand, and the better I paint.

Put several feeders with different seeds and suet near brushy cover outside your favorite window. Add a water drip nearby. With binoculars, field guide and sketch pad by your chair, you're on your way to sharpening your observation skills and, in turn, to becoming a better painter.

This photo was taken by my friend Deanne Fortnam in her wonderful terraced garden. Compare this shot with my final interpretation on the Goldfinch piece. Until I saw this picture, the idea of Goldfinches and yellow daisies had never occurred to me. Photo references are a first-rate resource.

Index